INFLUENCE, IMPACT & ETERNITY

Leadership Advice from the
West and the East on Missions

Dr. Neil Anderson

INFLUENCE, IMPACT & ETERNITY

Copyright © 2014 by Dr. Neil Anderson

All rights reserved. No part of this book may be reproduced or transmitted in any form or by any means without written permission of the author.

All Scripture quotations are taken from the New International Version of the Holy Bible (in the public domain.)

ISBN-13: 978-0-9904764-4-3

ISBN-10: 0-9904764-4-8

Library of Congress Control Number: 2014950209

Printed in the United States of America

RevMedia Publishing
PO BOX 5172
Kingwood, TX 77325

A publishing division of Revelation Ministries
www.revmediapublishing.com

Sowers Ministry
PO BOX 5148
Kingwood, TX 77325

sowers@aol.com
www.sowers.org

Cover Design by David Anderson

Editing assistance by Jeanette Morris, First Impressions Writing Services
www.firstimpressionswriting.com

Acknowledgement, appreciation and thanks:

This book is dedicated to all the leaders serving the Lord in difficult situation around the world.

I want to thank my wife, Amy, for her inspiration and encouragement to write this book. She helped with many hours of editing, researching, and the recordings of my life stories.

Also, much thanks to Christine Morgan for her work and time spent on this book and to Pastor Malcolm Burton for his expertise and editing experience. Thank you.

Foreword

We often read or hear persons referring to their dreams or visions. Years ago, my wife, Linda, and I went to China to smuggle Bibles to our persecuted Christian brethren there. That trip providentially brought Neil Anderson and his family into our lives. The Lord clearly merged our lives to Neil and The Sowers Ministry for the purpose of reaching millions of people in the 10/40 window of the world with the Word of God.

Over the years, we have been privileged to be a part of the Holy Spirit's reaching millions of the lost and saving them from eternal damnation. In addition, every year thousands of leaders are being discipled and trained to build strong churches.

The Lord is calling his people to help train up a new generation of leaders--young men and women who have a clear call of God on their lives, sound biblical teaching, practical training, and leadership skills. These new leaders will help establish and build the kingdom of God upon the earth. They will usher in a new wave that will see millions won to Christ, churches planted, Bible schools established, and more leaders trained.

By reading *Influence, Impact & Eternity*, leaders will be encouraged to train up the next generation of soul winners for Christ and plant churches. This book will give leaders the tools they need to influence and impact future generations for eternity.

Linda and I ask you to seek the Lord as to your dreams and visions to fulfill the Lord's commitment to reach the lost and usher them into His Kingdom of Everlasting Life!

Ray and Linda Goodrich
New York

Introduction

This book is about humble beginnings, life lessons, and God's triumphant victories in leaders' lives. For over twenty-eight years, I have traveled internationally planting, structuring, and funding The Sowers Ministry (TSM), a non-profit organization focusing on training Christian leaders and providing aid for the poor. We oversee thousands of churches. We house, feed, clothe, and educate orphans. Each year, we witness hundreds of thousands of decisions for Christ.

The focus of Sowers is to the most unreached areas of Asia. Our ministry is also to believers from Western nations, helping them discover and operate in their giftings when they travel abroad.

This book includes interviews with Asian leaders (names of individuals and locations may have been changed for reasons of personal security) who stand strong in the faith despite much persecution and hardship. Their stories motivate and inspire many people. I am fortunate to be able to have mentoring relationships with most of them as they continue to follow Jesus' example. I myself have experienced an improvement in my leadership skills by observing their persistence. For example, when I learn of a pastor serving in a prison labor camp for distributing Bibles, I push myself harder to travel, tell his story, and to raise awareness and prayer support to get him released and back into the pulpit.

As an influencer, I have learned to be open to others' input. God has many kinds of people. I live with flexibility to God's directions and sometimes make travel changes at the last minute. This is normal for a modern-day missionary and may even be critical for his/her safety. Training schedules are adjusted depending upon where I am in the world. Modeling these behaviors has helped to mature the Body of Christ, glorify Christ, and positively impact the quality of life for people groups internationally, I believe, for eternity.

In addition, this book contains advice and success stories from Western businessmen who have linked arms with TSM and are expanding the kingdom of God on earth. These individuals are also leaders in the Body of Christ who demonstrate their faith by funding gospel projects in remote parts of the world. The Sowers Ministry streams funding from churches and Christian businesses to native missionaries throughout Asia so that the unreached Muslim and Hindu areas of the world have the chance to hear about and receive Jesus. In turn, this opportunity blesses businesses, and I believe it provides protection for the nations that give resources for obeying Christ's Great Commission. Entrepreneurs do have the ability to save the world ... *in many effective ways.*

A brief review of leadership literature is also included, along with practical life skills, key actions, and character qualities. The examples presented include effective prayer, communicating well, problem-solving skills, edifying others, motivational secrets, maturity, humility, good financial stewardship, and mentoring. This combination of skills and disciplines are imperative to see godly order and divine influence happen. Yielding to God in these areas and denying ourselves helps leaders impact others more effectively. Along with possessing a servant's heart, these things can cause an unlocking of leadership in those who are being mentored. This usually results in an increase in church growth and yields positive, national changes.

My prayer is that this book will inform you regarding the subject of certain leadership behaviors...*especially in regards to influencing, impacting, praying for, and funding missions.* If everyone would get involved with the work of Christ, I believe the nations in the West could recover from financial hardship (Luke 6:38) and the third-world countries could be evangelized and walk in blessings, too. God is the God of the impossible. His prayer was for us to be one (John 17:21) and for His kingdom to come here on earth as it is in heaven. History has shown that as Christians unite, they are an eternal force for Christ. As we learn skills that also glorify Christ, like cultivating relationships, connecting to business professionals, and directing funds where most needed, we can witness positive community shifts and increased church growth in the West. I believe these are imperative things to do as we approach the return of Christ and the trying times that follow it.

There are many books written on leadership, but I have noticed that even though people know facts, often they do not model the behavior required. It is my prayer that I can present biblical lifestyle behaviors in an elementary format and share the passionate stories of missionaries living in persecuted areas to empower, to motivate, and to re-enforce how critical it is that we take the example of Christ's life seriously. Christ and His followers portray what is important in life and what produces lasting changes in us and for His kingdom in this world.

I also believe in impartation. I commit to agree in prayer for everyone who reads this book and applies this knowledge to his or her life. In the Bible, Jesus often gave instructions to people before the blessings manifested. As people obeyed Him, they received miracles. I have found that long-term success happens in the lives of obedient people.

As you read, learn, and apply the principles in this book, positive change will occur. Expectation is crucial. Think positive. These stories and the advice given are meant to inspire you while the instructions are meant to impart overcoming power to you.

Let us obey the Great Commission (Mark 16:15) together and watch increase happen.

CONTENTS

Chapter 1: Roots in Undefiled Religion..1
    Jing Min from China..3

Chapter 2: Monumental Change..7
    Motivation of Sister Chu in China...10
    Gang Member to Apostle: Brother Duan of China...................12
    Poverty to Full Provision, Sun Y. of China................................13

Chapter 3: Missions Leaders...19
    Testimony of M.P., owner of Bed & Breakfast.........................29
    Testimony of Sister D.Y.R. of China..30
    Reigning in Life: Pastor Wu...32
    Even So: Sister Sheng, Her Mother & the Gospel....................35

Chapter 4: Nations Need You 39
    Teaching by Entrepreneur M. Lewis..43
    Cyrus of Myanmar..45
    Changing his Nation by Discipleship: Sheng of Zheijiang.........46

Chapter 5: Taking Risks...49
    Das of India...54
    Persecuted Pastor Lee 55
    Unstoppable Wong..57
    Professor Bi of China 58
    Lamuel of India...60
    A Modern Day Apostle Paul, Li Wai...65

Chapter 6: Leadership & Agents of God..83
    Success Steps..83
    Developing Others..87
    Additional Leadership Advice..93
    Maturing in Leadership..95
    Missionary Lama of Tibet..99
    Touching Muslims with God's Love: Pastor Chan...................100

Chapter 7: Women on a Mission..103
    Testimony by Amy Anderson.......................................105
    Sister Bi on China and Influence..................................107
    Advice of Pastor Sikala of India 108
    Chao of Shanghai: Miracle, Prison, & Family Restored...........110
    Bible Women of Jilin, North China.............................112
    Thirty-eight Churches Planted and Counting: Shung H.S.........113

Chapter 8: Discipline, Money and Stewardship..............................115
    Legacy of Dr. P.P. Job by Neil Anderson...........................122
    Good and Faithful Servant: Jiang R. of China.....................124
    Despite Tragic Losses, the Wangs Kept their Faith................127
    Farmer's Family Delivered by the Hand of God in Vietnam......129

Chapter 9: Men Behind the Vision: Adopting Behaviors & Expecting
    Impartation...131
    Wade's Concrete Business, TX.......................................132
    R.W., President of H.A., Houston, TX.. ... .134
    MaryAnn Maciag, New York..135
    R. Garnett, London, UK..136
    Terry Chesbrough, Ft. Worth, TX.................................136
    Terry Barnett, TX...137
    Dr. Roger and Beverly Abel, FL.....................................138
    Dr. Paul Crites, Purpose International, TN.......................141

Chapter 1: Roots in Undefiled Religion

Neil's Testimony...

I was born and raised in the colorful and diverse country of India. When I was four, my young mother, who taught school in our village near Calcutta, died unexpectedly. As a result, my desperate and physically ill father decided to take my three brothers and I to a Methodist orphanage in West Bengal. Looking back, I am so thankful for my dad's Christian faith and for the pioneering Indian women who ran this work of God. But at the time, this loss of my parents was a great shock.

Back then, in 1960, women in my country were usually not so ambitious. But these ladies, lovingly nicknamed B.P. and C.P., traveled the world to raise funds so they could make a difference in the lives of children like me who probably would not have survived otherwise. They offered to raise us in the girls' hostel that they managed.

My financial support came from California. A Christian man who worked as a pilot provided for my basic needs and education. His support, which flowed through my legal caretakers, is largely why I survived. In addition, what he modeled played an important part in how I became who and what I am today.

Despite living in an orphanage, food was often inadequate. My immune system was weak. Because of this, I was often sick with fever and spent many dreadful days in the nurse's sick room. If I got a cut, it would always get infected. Even as a teenager, I lacked the food I needed to be healthy. In order to survive, I often stole vegetables from nearby gardens. Meat and sweets were rare and luxurious items. Clean water was similarly hard to find, especially during the summer. During the dry months, the government would bring rationed drinking water by the truckload. When that happened, a cold shower and a refreshing drink was the highlight of the day for everyone.

Soon I began plucking feathers from chickens for part-time work and managed to save a little money that way. In addition, I worked one day a week helping an ancient-looking man push a cart full of wheat to a local factory.

Otherwise, summertime was fun. I always looked forward to it because it was then that we would visit other orphanages and meet new friends. Living with other orphans enabled me to learn what it felt like to have a big family, as we actually lived just like brothers and sisters. Fishing, soccer, cricket, and other sports were favorite parts of my daily life.

The Methodist school I attended was named Ushagram. Today, school memories make me laugh. One time I had to jump out of the window to escape a spanking. We had an elderly teacher who would fall asleep and snore during the day. He would wake up angry and use a long stick to punish anyone in a front row seat. Ouch!

At the age of thirteen, a precious memory was made when I won first prize in my Sunday school for memorizing Scripture. In my childhood recollections, I recall how the minister there, Reverend Rosario, would pray extremely long and boring prayers. It was also during this time that I recall first hearing about two people who later made a profound impact on my faith life: Mother Theresa and the Assembly of God pastor in Calcutta, Mark Buntain.

Looking back, it is easy to see how the truth of Jeremiah 29:11 is evidenced in my testimony. God has a good plan for each individual's life, even for those starting life in an unfortunate circumstances. Despite my humble beginnings, God enabled me to rise above my challenges. Today, I live in prosperity and am able to help thousands of widows and orphans.

"Religion that God our Father accepts as pure and faultless is this: to look after orphans and widows in their distress and to keep oneself from being polluted by the world." (James 1:27) (7)

Keeping Valuable People Cared For

Every life is significant. History has been shaped by countless people who were originally orphans.

Moses, the first, and maybe most important leader of the Israelites, was originally an orphan. Alexander Hamilton, one of the Founding Fathers of the United States, and the thirty-first president of the United States, Herbert Hoover, were orphans.

One of the greatest inventors of all time, George Washington Carver, was an orphan. Johann Sebastian Bach, Edgar Allen Poe, Aristotle, Leo Tolstoy, Percy Spencer…were all orphans. The list of famous orphans goes on and on—parentless men and women who grew up to become politicians, actors, athletes, playwrights, and televisions producers.

No life is disposable. Everyone is valuable. No matter what, a person can become a major contributor to society, and more importantly, to God's kingdom-building work.

Each of us can do things to help an orphan child become all he/she can be in this life. Donations to reputable agencies are the most practical way to help them. Other crucial contributions that are needed by orphans are prayers, hugs, and words of encouragement. The child you hug may grow up to be a world-changer and even achieve fame in the kingdom of God.

Today, I have a heart for orphans in many parts of the world, including China and North Korea. The following is a true story:

Jing Min from China

Jing Min has lived on the streets for as long as he can remember. As a little boy, he was abandoned by his parents and left homeless, alone, and unwanted. He wandered around the streets and alleys of Sanyuan County for four long years before he was finally picked up by a local and brought to the orphanage. When the staff members heard of his ordeals on the street, they were speechless with disbelief. Multiple times Jing had been tied up to lampposts by strangers and he underwent long periods of illness due to severe weather and a weak immune system.

When Jing was brought to the orphanage he was filthy and had long, matted hair. He never properly learned to use and go to the restroom, so he often urinated and defecated into his pants. The first time Jing was bathed, a gigantic wound was found on his right arm where an elastic cord was digging into his muscles. He was immediately sent to the hospital where doctors recommended amputation of his arm. The procedure would cost about 2,000 RMB ($400 USD). Jing understood the meaning of an amputation and begged the medical team to find a way to keep his arm. After further examination and testing, Jing's doctor pointed out that he could keep his arm, but it would cost him 7,000 RMB ($1400 USD).

Miraculously, donations made to the orphanage made it possible for surgeons to work on his arm. He is now recovering at the orphanage, has a positive outlook on life, and has already made many friends.

Please keep Jing in your prayers and support him as he will have future surgery expenses in order to treat his arm. He will remain at the orphanage until he goes out in search for a job and becomes independent. Meanwhile, he is learning to properly read and write, and so far, he has been doing very well in school. The best news, however, is that he has learned about the love of God and accepted Jesus into his heart. Wherever life takes him, he now knows that he will never have to face the streets on his own again because Christ lives within him. Though he was once abandoned and left to fend for himself, he is now aware that he has a Heavenly Father who is watching over him and a new family at the orphanage that loves him dearly.

Chapter 2: Monumental Change

Neil's Testimony continues…

During my teenage years, I attended a Christian, revival meeting. My spirit awakened and got in tune with God. But months later, I drifted away because of the pressures of the world.

I now recall physical hunger was a constant problem that made it difficult to concentrate in school. Soon I found myself hanging out at the movie theatre in my city where I befriended a young man who taught corrupt business dealings. Because of the young man's influence, I quickly learned the behavior modeled in front of me. When I was only seventeen, I entered the business world selling aquariums. Later I made money by bribing auctioneers that sold coal and I would resell it at two or three times what it was worth—something like scalping tickets for sporting events.

In college, I found it very hard to concentrate because I believed I was gifted in the field of business and this was where I should be investing my time. My ability to make money often caused me to miss class.

Business success made me feel like I was somebody important. This pull between business and education was extremely stressful. During my chemistry exam, I broke down and began crying. I was the last person to leave the classroom, but I did eventually graduate with a Bachelors of Science degree.

Business then became a way of life for me. As I observed other businessmen, I noticed how they spoke and convinced myself that I could do even better. Before long, I found out that I was right. My investments grew larger and larger.

Favor was extended to me by a very successful man who mentored me. Waves of business patterns and connections began to develop around me.

Suddenly, one of my business partners, a friend of my father, died. I was close to him and this brought great sadness and pondering into my life. This caused me to think about the corrupt business practices I was engaged in. I decided I wanted to change for the better.

In my heart I knew that eventually everyone reaps what they sow. During this time, I also experienced a huge disappointment when I lent a large sum of money to a friend who never paid me back.

"All my dirty business deals have come back to bite me," I thought to myself. I did not throw the baby out with the bathwater, though. I still had a drive to do business and make things happen. Every time I saw business skills demonstrated in front of me, I knew it was what I was created to do.

Shortly after these disappointing events, I was invited by an American family to spend time with them in Nepal. By then my brother, Guine, was a missionary. He lived with a missionary family and helped plant churches. This family had faithfully written several letters to me each week, always expressing how they cared for me. This went on for several years. This is my strongest memory of real, parental love. So I decided to go to Nepal.

There, on a Saturday morning in 1982 I rededicated my life to Jesus Christ. I distinctly remember Matthew 6:33 being spoken in the sermon that day. It says, "But seek first his kingdom and his righteousness, and all these things will be given to you as well" (7).

I lived with the American family for six months while pondering my next move. I witnessed and received so much love from this family that I finally decided to forsake all my past achievements. I gave up everything. I left behind my money and six years of business deals in

Chapter 2: Monumental Change

India, *and surrendered my life to God*. Just a few days later, I was baptized in the freezing cold, mountain water of the Himalayas.

My life had taken a *monumental change*. Instead of doing business, I found myself teaching math in a Christian elementary school. Later on, I landed a job as a computer technician at the United Nations.

God then provided an opportunity for me to travel to Hong Kong and later to America for an even greater commissioning. I accepted God's calling on my life. It came on my brothers' lives as well. In Nepal, we attended church seven days a week for three years. Ninety-nine percent of the time, I would be the first person to arrive to the service. My American host family was of the Baptist denomination and frowned upon anyone being late or missing church. Because it was so new to me, I considered attending church a fun thing to do. Special pleasure was derived from hearing and learning the English language too. This proved to be a maturing phase of my life as I learned to draw peace and wisdom directly from the Holy Spirit of God. This would prove to be a crucial skill that carries me throughout life.

Then in 1985, I read the international best-selling book by missionary Richard Wurmbrand called *Tortured for Christ*. The book spoke of the faithfulness of Christians enduring great persecution in China, Romania, Russia, and the Eastern European nations.

Soon after reading the book, I also attended a service hosted by Rev. Wurmbrand. He repeatedly asked the question, "Who will go to the communist nations?" After that, I met another man who was very close to Wurmbrand, Dr. P.P. Job. As a foot soldier for Jesus, I was sometimes kidnapped or beaten up by unbelievers. I daily surrender my life to Christ.

My heart was particularly stirred by a teaching about idol worship from Psalm 115:2-8 that states, "Why do the nations say, 'Where is their God?' Our God is in heaven; he does whatever pleases him. But their idols are silver and gold, made by human hands. They have mouths, but cannot speak, eyes, but cannot see. They have ears, but cannot hear, noses, but cannot smell. They have hands, but cannot feel, feet, but cannot walk, nor can they utter a sound with their throats. Those who make them will be like them, and so will trust in them." (7) I thought to myself, "If I don't share the good news of Jesus Christ, God is going to get angry."

My trip to America included a visit to Lakewood Church and meeting Pastor John Osteen, who was so in tune with the Holy Spirit. This is where I soon became ordained and a part of the huge evangelizing machine God was building. This was a time of explosive spiritual growth for me as I learned that Scripture states our actions can hasten the day of the Lord (2 Peter 3:12). This is responsibility!

My belief is that when God looks at a nation, He looks mostly for the evidence of undefiled religion in practice: caring for orphans and widows. God truly turned me, a nobody, into somebody in a key position to further His kingdom through this model. If Christ dwells in us, we are royalty and anything is possible!

Now that I have shared more about my humble beginnings, I want to share some stories of Christian sisters and brothers in China. These dedicated believers inspire me to be the best minister/leader and missionary I can be.

Motivation of Sister Chu of China

Sister Chu is eighty-four years old and she is *still* a passionate Christian. Even at this advanced age, Sister Chu is a prominent leader of the China house church movement as she continues to travel to various locations to preach and to teach the Word of God.

However, life has not always been easy for her. Chu was imprisoned for twenty-five years for her faith, and during that time, her husband left her for another woman. She even had to take her young son into the prison with her because there was no one to look after him.

Chapter 2: Monumental Change

Sister Chu was imprisoned in to the Northeastern part of China, close to the Siberian border. It was freezing cold there. On occasion, temperatures dropped to -40 degrees F. She dug through the snow to get grass roots to feed herself and her son, who was only three years old at the time. Often, she carried heavy loads of debris on her shoulders or swept the floor of the prison for many hours.

The guards shaved Sister Chu's head and forced her to carry a board across her should blades with the words "I am a Christian" written on it. Many times, Chu would bleed from sores on different areas of her body.

Eventually, she fell ill but the other prisoners had compassion on her and looked after her son. Chu consistently prayed to the Lord to take care of her son, Moses. He became a source of joy and strength to many women while they were imprisoned.

After twenty-five years, the prison officials admitted that they had been wrong to send Chu to prison. She was released, and her confiscated home and belongings were returned back to her.

However, the hardship continued. Her daughter and her son-in-law were also sent to prison on four different occasions. Revival was occurring and they were in charge of over fifty house churches at one time!

Persecution and imprisonment will never stop Chu though. She continues to preach the good news. Despite being badly beaten in prison, she would not deny her faith in Jesus. She told the police that her faith in Him was more important than being released from prison. Her life experiences have led her to this conclusion: "Persecution is the beginning of revival fire in China." Today, her son is grown and pastors his own churches.

Pastor Chu has since started several teaching programs to train up more church leaders. Although she is elderly now, by the grace of God, she is still strong and able to minister! She believes and declares that our lives are to reflect Jesus. He obeyed His Father and we are to follow His example.

She is also able to deliver thousands of Bibles and teaching books to many of the underground house churches all over China. Because of the lack of Bibles and the immense population, many believers must share a copy. It is not unusual to hear of one Bible being shared by many believers!

Last year, Sister Chu led two hundred people to Jesus. She also trained nearly 1,300 leaders. God has helped her to start many churches...each ranging between 80 to 300 believers. She now travels to many locations and teaches in 2,000 house churches all over China!

Chu's life is an example of how God can use tough times to refine the church just like fire purifies gold. Our God strengthens those who are willing to follow Him. He reignites the flames of revival. Please pray for the thousands of Chinese gospel workers who are ministering with Chu. She is like Nehemiah in the Bible. Sister Chu is a great example of a church planter. Her faithful efforts have resulted in massive church growth in China.

Gang Member to Apostle: Brother Duan of China

Brother Duan of China was a former gang leader who frequented prison because of his activities. He also suffered physically and lost much of his sight for almost three years. He had to wear expensive glasses.

After twenty years of poor health, a Christian sister shared the gospel with Duan and invited him to a church meeting. There the believers ministered and prayed over him. After three days, Duan was healed. He gave his life to Jesus and never looked back. Duan has since seen many miracles in his own life and ministry.

He was arrested in July 2004 because his illegal church had grown to over 1,200 members. He was interrogated, beaten, and tortured for several days. The first two weeks of his imprisonment were, to say the least, hellacious.

His prison cell conditions were far worse than those of other prisoners. He was so intensely tortured that the other inmates questioned him about what crime he had committed. After confessing to being a believer and follower of Christ, he was mocked and ridiculed by the other prisoners.

Despite the hardship, Brother Duan kept on trusting the Lord. Eventually, his fellow inmates were saved and he was moved to a larger cell to serve out his sentence. Much of this time, he interceded for other believers and the church in Lailoling province. His trials strengthened him and brought him great joy. He is always seeking God and expanding his churches. (To date, Brother Duan has to date planted over 1,000 churches around Dalian and Anhui.) Greater things are yet to come!

Poverty to Full Provision, Sun Y. of China

Four hours from the provincial capital city of Shenyang, China, is the beautiful mountain village of Liaoning where Sun Y. was born in February of 1970. He was the youngest of thirteen children.

When he was born, Sun Y. was so underweight and small that his parents thought that there was no way they could help him. They thought that his was a hopeless case, and he would not be able to survive.

Born into poverty where life was very hard for his parents, his mother figured that the only solution was to kill him. She decided to suffocate him with a cotton quilt.

The next morning, his mother uncovered him and found he was still alive.

She was still determined to kill Sun Y. and went to cover him again. Just as she was about to put the quilt over him again, she saw a man dressed in a white gown appear before her saying, "Don't kill him. Bring him up [raise him], I want him to serve Me!"

His mother was shocked but she obeyed. She let her son live and raised him.

Before 1949 and the Communist takeover, Sun Y.'s father was a wealthy landlord. After communism was instated, his family was declared to be "Enemy Class" and they faced much persecution. During the Cultural Revolution, three of his siblings died.

During the Cultural Revolution, an internal war that lasted from 1966-1976, the authorities used a rebellious gang called the Red Guards to further the revolution. The Red Guards came and took away all their property.

The family became so poor that Sun Y. did not even have a pair of trousers to wear to school! He had to borrow his sister's while she stayed home covered in a blanket. He did not get his own trousers until he was sixteen!

At sixteen, he could not stand the way he was living. He hated how poverty forced them to live in such horrible conditions.

As a solution to his problems, Sun Y. decided to become a thief. He did not take from the local villagers, but decided only to steal from the government.

He took food, building materials, and other useful items. The village, however, was too small and he was left unsatisfied. He wanted more.

Sun Y. gathered a group of sixteen like-minded individuals and formed a gang that elected him as leader. They raided government buildings and even freight trains. Sun Y. would jump on the train and throw the goods down to his people who would take them to sell in the black market.

Soon, they became rich–millionaires!

Chapter 2: Monumental Change

He lived the rich life, enjoying his wealth. Women started to flirt with him and demand his attention. Although he married in 1992, he kept four lovers. He took turns living with these different women. His new status did not bring him the satisfaction he thought he would gain. He had no peace and no joy.

Sun Y. also lived in fear. The authorities were after him. One day, the police found him and he was arrested. He was left with only one officer to watch him, as the other police went after his partners. He was able to attack the policeman and escape.

Sun Y. had a sister who was nineteen years older than he was. She was a Christian and was constantly pleading with him to give up his criminal ways and turn himself in to the authorities. He was still fearful. Sun Y. had learned that the sentence for his crimes was fourteen years. He did not want to go to prison. He already knew what a hard life looked like.

Despite his fear, his sister insisted on his surrender and promised to organize her church members to pray for him. In 1996, Sun Y. astonished the chief of police by turning himself in. He was still fearful, but his conscience would not let him have peace, and his new life never offered true joy.

The chief of police detained him, handcuffing his hands and feet, for good measure. He was told that he would stay in jail for fourteen days until they could take him to court and convict him.

After fourteen days, the chief of police came to negotiate. "We know that you are head of the thieves' gang," said the chief. "If you can persuade your people to surrender, we will set you all free." Sun Y. agreed and with his help, the other gang members all turned themselves in. The chief kept his word and set them all free. Sun Y. later found out that during those fourteen days in jail, his sister and her church were praying for him. He saw firsthand how God was sovereign in his situation. He knew it was God who helped him.

After Sun Y. gave his life to Christ, he dedicated himself to learning more about the Bible. He is committed to serving God and His people.

Sun Y. says he has found the joy he was searching for all his life. Surrendering his life to Christ has made Sun Y.'s relationships better as well.

After he was saved, his wife forgave him. He and his wife enjoy the life they share with their two beautiful daughters.

Sun Y. separated himself from his mistresses. Before doing so, he gave them $30,000 each. God used Sun Y.'s changed lifestyle to minister to the women. Now, two of them have become believers. Brother Sun Y. also witnessed to his family, and all of his siblings are believers as well.

His walk with Jesus is a testimony to the people who knew him before his life was changed. Many people come to him, wanting to hear about Jesus testifying, "No one could change Sun Y., but God did. The God who Sun Y. believes in must be the true one!"

Sun Y.'s changed life has influenced the villagers so much that crime rates have decreased. There is no gambling, theft, or fighting in his village.

Sun Y.'s ministry has continued to grow. The village leaders were so pleased with the changes happening in the village they offered him a nice, 66,000 sq. ft. building to use as a home church. Originally, about 100 people met there regularly. Sun Y. was invited to share his testimony with other villages and now his church serves over 900 believers!

Sun Y. and his team train youth leaders to serve the Lord, and they also supply Bibles to rural areas. He has requested more Bibles in preparation for the day when God answers his prayer that they reach more people with the gospel. He hopes to equip more new believers to grow strong in their faith and become effective as well.

Sun Y. says that Jesus brought him out of poverty, not just materially, but spiritually. He testifies about a life free of fear and full of joy. He holds to the Scripture in John, where Jesus says, "I am the bread of life. He who comes to me will never go hungry, and he who believes in me will never be thirsty... Whoever drinks the water I give him will never thirst" (John 6:35). "Indeed the water I give him will become in him a spring of water welling up to eternal life" (John 4:14) (7).

Chapter 3: Missions Leaders

More of Neil's testimony...

After my salvation and infilling with the Holy Spirit, God began to grow my desire to travel to the borders of China and Tibet. My brothers and I traveled there and engaged in prayer walks for these nations. Atmospheres change for the better when Christians physically go to the place that God directs them to and then pray there. During those years, I traveled great distances to go to the boundaries of these closed, most often communist, nations, and as often as I could, stepped over into those territories in order to claim the nations for Jesus by praying and speaking God's love and peace.

Sometimes this boldness appeared to be life threatening. On one occasion, armed guards bearing guns arrested us at the Chinese border. But nothing could extinguish the fire God had placed in me to make a difference in Asian nations.

The story of Sadhu Sunder Singh greatly motivated me to become a missionary. Brother Singh was a Sikh disciple of a guru. This amazing man became a Christian because he had a dream in which God stood in front of him and told him where to go.

Brother Singh walked great distances in the frozen Himalayan Mountains, without wearing shoes, *just to bring the gospel to Tibet*. These kinds of missionary stories really inspired me to continue my calling.

Nepal Miracle

Just as biblical heroes of the Old Testament would remember past victories to inspire their faith, I like to think of God and all the blessings

He has bestowed on me throughout the years. This also propels my motivation. His miracles fuel me to endure hardship and to help others.

One example occurred in the 1980s in the tiny country of Nepal, just north of India. Back then, no one in that part of the world had ever seen a computer, yet God performed a miracle through us and an Australian businessman when twenty computers were transferred as gifts from Hong Kong without us having to pay any taxes!

This caused the Nepali people to really notice the favor of God upon the prayers of my brothers and I. God had provided divine connections to enable this to happen. These links are often the difference between ministries that make a huge difference in the world and ministries that do not. Every day I believe and thank God for His divine connections.

China and Tibet

After years of prayer, China and Tibet became accessible to me. The first time I saw and learned of these unique people groups, I was intrigued. The diligence of Chinese construction workers made a big impression on me. They never even sat down while eating their lunches. They quickly slurped up their noodles with chopsticks and went back to work! Located in the center of Asia, Tibet is surrounded by the Himalayas to the west, south, and east, and the Kunluns to the north. These mountains, some of them up to 22,000 feet high, have proven to be an almost impassable barrier to conquering armies, traders, migratory peoples, adventurers, and missionaries. The dry landscape, most of which is over 15,000 feet high include the Salween river gorges that provide some access for travelers. As a result, Tibet has been isolated from the outside world's influences, including Christianity, for centuries.

Pressured by freezing winters and dry summers, Tibet's two million inhabitants fight for survival. Nomads herding yaks and sheep dot the landscape. Yaks pull ploughs on the few existing farms. In the villages, which are few and far between, people live in flat-roofed mud houses. They use rancid-smelling yak butter for just about everything -- as a skin protector, a tea drink, or an offering to idols. They speak a common language, which is similar to Burmese. Tibetans believe that they will go to hell to pay for their sins before being reincarnated. Few of them have ever heard about the Son of God, who has already paid for those sins. (16-20)

The amazing beauty of the Tibetan womens' dresses are another sight to behold. While in those two countries, I often felt like I was on another planet! Then there is the cuisine of these cultures... *absolutely exotic, but sometimes even repulsive to the mind of a businessman.*

With time and experience, I have learned to appreciate most of the cultural practices of these people whom God loves with an everlasting love. Despite the differences between us, the Lord gave me an eternal heart to reach them that included the grace to release anointing and communicate love without knowing their language fluently and to eat all kinds of their food. Food is considered a very special gift when these people prepare it for a foreigner. Their trust in me seemed to increase more quickly when I ate with them.

I can still remember more powerful images imprinted upon my mind about the gruesome way the Tibetans disposed of their dead. Read the following excerpt for an example: Your mother has just died. Fortunately, the Podeb is here. He yanks the hair from the top of her head, freeing her spirit from her body to go into the next mortal – man or animal, you are not sure which. What if her spirit stays around the house instead of departing? Fortunately, the Joba, can prevent that. He carries her body to some deserted spot. There he chops her body up and spreads the internal organs out, attracting vultures and wolves by eating some of her flesh himself. Later, some of her bones are used for fertilizer or carved into religious objects or musical instruments.

Is this some gruesome horror story? No. These are scenes from Tibet, a nation long steeped in ignorance, demonism and Tibetan Buddhism, called Lamaism. This nation is in desperate need of hearing the truth of the gospel of Jesus Christ (16-20).

However, I learned that through the Buddhist promise of better reincarnations leading to Nirvana, Satan has enslaved the people to a life-time preoccupation with right words and works. "Om Mani Padme Hun" (Om, the Jewel in the Lotus) and other phrases chanted repeatedly to false gods who can supposedly stop the cycle of reincarnations and help the speaker enter Nirvana immediately. The phrases found on the walls in every town, are inserted thousands of times into prayer wheels. People walk through the towns, spinning the wheels, thereby releasing millions of prayers that lead them, supposedly, to a hastier Nirvana. Prayer flags release the phrases every time they flap in the breeze. Every Tibetan owns a rosary; the worshipper recites Buddha's name 100 times. Actually, the rosary has 108 beads – eight extra in case the devotee forgets a prayer or loses his beads.

The Dalai Lama is chosen during the first year of his life by means of rites involving witchcraft; the Tibetans see him as their savior. They believe he has sacrificed himself on their behalf, "…Voluntarily re-entering the world of suffering, binding himself to it [and postponing release into Nirvana], until he has ultimately brought them all to the state of bliss he has won for himself." The Tibetans do not know Jesus, the true Savior who justifies them by His blood and frees them from guilt and bondage to good works.

The Light shines in the darkness…Jesus Christ is the King of the world.

Mission work into Tibet has been agonizing and almost non-existent, due to the harsh Tibetan landscape coupled with the Dalai Lama's fear of loss of power from foreign intruders. Two Jesuit priests succeeded in penetrating Tibet in 1661. In 1745, Tibetan Lamas expelled some of the Jesuits. In the 1800's, Tibetan borders were slammed shut in fear of foreigners interested in Tibetan gold and in changing Tibetan religion. One missionary, Annie Taylor, managed to get within three days journey to Lhasa, only to be arrested. Always missionaries faced difficult journeys, and some have lost their lives due to harsh Tibetan landscape and climate. Faced with perilous journeys, certain difficult living conditions, and threat of persecution, Christians don't want to go there.

Yet, there is today light in Tibet, strong signs that God is moving with His Holy Spirit. According to a report in China and the Church Today from Gansu province, an area worked extensively by several missions groups before the communists came to power, a few Christian households had gathered together to worship during a Chinese New Year's celebration (20). Their neighbors, seeking to wipe out Christianity, disrupted their meeting and told them to disperse. The Christians, unwilling to stop their meeting, were severely beaten by the crowd. The next morning, their persecutors found their herds of sheep, cows, and horses dying. Their family members began to die one by one. Realizing that the wrath of God had fallen upon them, they pleaded with those who believed in Jesus to pray. The Lord heard the believer's prayers, and the sick and the dying were healed. As a result, more than a hundred Tibetans turned to the Lord! (16-20)

Initially, I believe freedom for the Tibetan people came partly through missionaries like my brothers, Guine and Sandy, Dr P.P. Job and me. Tibetans traditionally prostrate their bodies on the floor to worship idols. This is what they originally thought freedom was. But, God gave me a message when they asked me what my God thought about this practice. Under the inspiration of the Holy Spirit, I told them their idols were blind gods who could not help them get back up and stand strong. The Scripture God gave me was, "The idols of the nations are silver and gold, made by human hands. They have mouths, but cannot speak, eyes, but cannot see. They have ears, but cannot hear, nor is there breath in their mouths. Those who make them will be like them, and so will all who trust in them," (Psalm 135:15-18)(7).

Through this evangelization and teaching experience, I learned that the poorest people are usually the most spiritually vulnerable. Tragic circumstances, usually involving witchcraft, can often be a result.

The Bible reveals what we know to be the Great Commission: "Therefore go and make disciples of all nations, baptizing them in the name of the Father and of the Son and of the Holy Spirit" (Matthew 28:19)(7). The Word of God also states, "Your kingdom come, your will be done, on earth as it is in heaven" (Matthew 6:10)(7).

In my opinion, these two verses summarize the purity and whole gospel of Jesus Christ. All Christians should play a part in God's plan to do exactly this. When we study the life of Christ, we see it was a fulfilling one. He desires to give that abundant life to every person ... *to you* and *through you*. What a joy to have Christ in our hearts and manifesting through our lives so that people around us can have that fullness too.

As I write these words, I am reminded of the time when Jesus described the call to ministry that rested upon His life by quoting Old Testament scripture: "The Spirit of the Lord is on me, because he has anointed me to proclaim good news to the poor. He has sent me to proclaim freedom for the prisoners and recovery of sight for the blind, to set the oppressed free" (Luke 4:18)(7).

Disasters in 2009, like the severe earthquake that hit China's Sichuan Province, the flooding in Myanmar, and the tsunamis in Thailand and India, forced many to live in hardship and suffering. Hundreds and thousands were killed who had not received Jesus. In fact, most of these individuals died without having even heard His Name once!

Often I ask myself, "Will those who survived these disasters and other unreached people groups ever get a chance to hear the good news and hope in Christ before another catastrophe occurs?"

Everyone should have a chance to repent. As we know in the West, many people need to hear the gospel a few times before they accept Jesus.

The world is desperate for Christ. Many children have to do unthinkable things like work and live in garbage dumps in order to survive! All around Asia, children sell their parents' blood, or are even themselves sold by their parents to be prostitutes in Hindu temples.

Loan sharks will gladly buy children because their parents cannot afford to take care of them. This is all to put food on the table or worse yet—*to fund drug and alcohol abuse*. Many family members each sell their kidneys to support their family.

The more of the world that I see, the larger the vision I have for the millions in Asia who are lost and have no hope. This is a normal reaction according to Scripture, "...where sin increased, grace increased all the more...," (Romans 5:20). Matthew 25:40 reveals the heart of God in this matter: "The King will reply, 'Truly I tell you, whatever you did for one of the least of these brothers and sisters of mine, you did for me.'" (7)

Making Things Happen

Christ's last command is our first concern. It is found in Mark 16:15. His commission is to witness to the entire world. In order to participate in the worldwide perspective, we must understand the function of missions. Jesus has given us instructions that concern the importance of reaching everyone with the gospel. The world is filled with people whose faith has diminished and who are desperately seeking love and understanding, both of which can only flow through Jesus Christ.

We must be willing to be used like tools for the functioning of His kingdom coming on earth. We must be focused upon the harvest in order to be used in the mission field. Thank the Lord for what He has done, is doing, and will continue to do until His eternal purpose is manifested.

We experience Him at work in a world that is lost and seeking atonement between man and God. We also have a huge responsibility to disciple new believers. When we see the enormity of the task, we are inclined to grow faint, or even fail at times.

However, once we become committed to God's task, then we see the ministry of missions as our privilege.

A Leader's Motivation

Many Christian leaders ask, "What is God's calling and will for my ministry?" Yes, it is important to line up with God's purpose, Word, and Spirit so that He can impart His plan, goals, and objectives for each individual believer and ministry.

Everyone understands the meaning of carrying a heavy burden. A burden is not bought at a store, sent in the mail, or even obtained at a seminary. A burden is that divine act of God in which He puts His concern or feeling on your heart. It could be about a specific area in your life, a people group, or a geographical location. You actually begin to feel how the Lord feels toward it.

If God is concerned about something, you, as a believer, should have the same feeling, concern, and willingness to do what you can to bring about change. But I have found you cannot have an equal burden for every part of the world. Instead, God calls specific people for specific places. When He puts a burden for a particular area of the world on your heart, then that burden starts to develop. When it does, you begin to analyze what God wants you to do about it. When you are dedicated and willing to lay down your life to see God's work done, then we call it, "having a burden." This is the divine act of God that many missionaries, who have gone before us, have experienced. They were motivated to "go."

There has never been a better leader than Jesus Christ. What was his style? Jesus led by the greatest example possible: by being a servant to those around Him.

The most beautiful and exciting picture of Jesus in the Bible is that of Him hanging upon the cross. Yet, His second most meaningful action was when He walked into the room, looked at His followers, and began to wash their feet. He understood a servant's heart and thus, leadership! He was illustrating to his disciples how to treat enemies and showing them that leadership meant having a heart to carry other people's burdens.

A leader genuinely cares for others. Some examples of this are: Mother Theresa of Calcutta, a city that is located near the area where I am originally from. Late Pastor John Osteen of Houston, TX, led his congregation to make enormous contributions to world missions. Reinhard Bonnke's healing and salvation messages have brought and are still bringing millions of souls to Jesus. The Billy Graham Evangelistic Association has reached billions with a simple gospel message and an invitation.

Early in my ministry, my vision included printing the true gospel for people via "The Lighthouse" publishers and through audio tapes. God helped these two vehicles of communication to get into thousands of homes every month.

Mission leaders are desperately needed today. A true leader hears God's voice, acts upon it, and continues in a firm relationship with the Father. I recently learned that out of every $100 given to mission work, only one cent is given to those individuals who work among the 3.5 billion unreached people groups in the 10/40 window of the world. Jesus spoke of today in Matthew 9:37-38 when He stated, "Then he said to his disciples, 'The harvest is plentiful but the workers are few. Ask the Lord of the harvest, therefore, to send out workers into his harvest field'" (7).

Today, The Sowers Ministry is doing just what Jesus instructed us to do back then by sending out national missionaries.

During one period of my life, I lived in a rural setting in Europe. While I was there, I observed how the farmers' tractor combines would collect the harvest of an entire field. Likewise, Christians today must also reach the unreached people groups of the world.

While in rural Europe, I saw how farmers sow seed into fertile ground. The result is a quick and healthy harvest! On the other hand, we cannot forget places like North Korea where the ground still seems quite hard. This country may take much preparatory humanitarian work (e.g., seven years worth) before it is ready for the gospel.

North Korea is on my heart. I have observed them harvesting their corn, wheat, soy, and other grains. Some doors are opening up there per my observations. This is motivating for me. My prayer is to sow seed and to see a spiritual harvest take place.

Missions Begin with a Vision from God

What does it mean to have a vision? A vision is a picture of what God wants you to be or to do. Focusing on a vision enables us to watch that vision grow in our own lives. As the vision grows within us, we are then able to plant the same vision into someone else's heart. A vision not only needs to be in your mind, but it must be written down so that you can pray about it more specifically.

To me, a genuine leader is one who has a vision that includes a sense of God's vision of evangelistic outreaches. A vision comes together when we spend time in God's Word and presence.

Faith is another aspect of a vision, because it is that which separates the natural structure from the divine structure saying, "I am going to reach out to a lost and hurting world." The Bible says it is the power of God that enables us to do the will of the Lord, and we need His power and anointing to do the job that has been appointed to us.

May His Holy Spirit and gifts dwell in us so that we can do His mighty tasks as leaders with faith and vision!

Let me share some powerful testimonies. One is from a businessman who funds TSM. Others are from influential Chinese pastors and believers. All are important in the kingdom of God, because some send and some go.

Testimony of M. P., owner of a Christian Bed and Breakfast

I own a Christian B&B and I believe in working hard for the kingdom of God. I have a heart for and am humbled to be a part of genuine missions work. God gripped my heart for missions work fifteen years ago when I attended a conference at the Astrodome, and I saw a booth supporting missionaries that go into many diverse parts of the world. God touched me in that moment and I immediately broke down sobbing. I knew I had to get involved.

At that time, I was employed as a General Manager of Hewlett Packard. My schedule was a busy one but I signed up to go on a mission trip to Bangladesh.

Bangladesh was 88 percent Muslim, 11 percent Hindu, and only 0.3 percent Christian. I was part of a team tasked with training believers. During the time there, we imparted Bible truths to 250 men and 50 women. I can honestly say the Holy Spirit taught through me.

We were also able to baptize former Muslims. This left a lasting impression on me knowing that they would most likely be shunned, beaten, or even killed because of their conversion to Christianity.

We baptized 100 people. As I participated in the baptisms, I looked into the eyes of each individual, knowing full well what waited for them.

Like many others, I am blessed to be part of God's plan for the work of the Great Commission by fueling those who do. I do not travel abroad and do mission work anymore, but I can fund those who can go.

In my heart, I believe what mission workers do is what I call priestly ministry. Businessmen and women such as I serve in the kingship roles that support the priests. I operate in the power to get wealth in order to fund mission work and to provide needed resources throughout the world. I am drawn to operate in kingship responsibilities. This is my calling.

Along the way, I have learned some principles. Wherever we store up treasures, there is our heart also, and what we cast upon the water comes back to us. Money is power and power accomplishes things. Money can cause good people to become better or bad people to become worse.

At the end of my life, I do not want to report my savings account amount to God. Hopefully, I can say that I followed the gifting God gave to me and did what He instructed me to do.

Testimony of Sister D.Y.R., China

I was raised in a Christian family and lived my life as a faithful Christian. One night in 1973, God spoke and called me to give my life over to His service. I was immediately motivated to go and started teaching in Christian gatherings in surrounding areas.

While doing so, I encouraged believers to live a godly life and surrender all to Jesus. I also started walking, sometimes fifteen miles one way, to mountain villages to preach the gospel and teach believers. Then, during the 1976 Cultural Revolution in China, life became extremely difficult and many Christians were imprisoned for being followers of Jesus Christ.

Chapter 3: Missions Leaders

In 1978, I started a church and many people came to know the Lord. We had only one Bible for the whole church to read. Some borrowed the Bible and copied chapter by chapter by hand. During the period between 1980 and 1990, countless believers were tortured and sent to labor camps. Some of my own gospel workers had to go to these camps and two of them died while there.

Persecution brought fear into some churches. However, a move of the Holy Spirit began to touch lives and many were healed. Miracles were taking place everywhere. It seemed to me as if the Books of Acts was actually happening.

By 1994, we had about 400 members in our church. That is when the police started to persecute us. Every week they broke up our meetings and dispersed the congregation.

The officers warned us to stop having religious gatherings. We ignored them and followed the Lord's instructions. The congregation continued to gather to worship God and to pray together.

Soon the police raided our meetings, dispersed the people, and confiscated all our Bibles and songbooks. They used a big van to take away all of our furniture.

After prayer, the Lord guided us to meet in smaller groups to avoid unnecessary attention from the police. One year later, the police again started raiding our small gatherings and, once again, confiscated our belongings. I was forced to pay heavy fines for the "illegal gatherings."

The church grew in spite of these persecutions. One night, the police came in, took me out of the house, and put me into prison. No bail was set. No visitation was allowed with my family. No one knew my whereabouts. I was kept in a dark and freezing cold place. The guards gave me old food and very little of that. I lost a lot of weight and began to question God. Most of all, I was worried about my husband and my children.

One day, as I sat in the dark prison room, the Lord spoke to me. I began to cry for forgiveness. He reminded me of the apostle Paul who went through persecution as he was used by the Lord.

God promised me that He would use me as well. I had to work very hard in prison, but after long hours of work, I always found the time to pray. I had opportunities to share my faith with the other women. Often, they comforted me and hugged me when they learned of my sorrow and how much I missed my children.

One morning, after I got ready for work, the police came to my cell and said, "You are free to go home."

My prison sentence had been three and a half years. Actually, the detainment was more like a cruel army training camp.

Through this, the Lord prepared me to serve Him better and to discover that life is wonderful.

Today, the churches I oversee are compelled to go to unreached people groups. They have grown in passion for the Lord and in number with great signs and wonders as well as healings among the people. In Matthew 16:18 Jesus reminds us, "I will build my church." (7)

Our churches are making huge differences in two provinces. Thousands are turning to Christ each year in these areas and are motivated to go and evangelize.

My vision is to reach the people in every mountain village of one province in particular and to bring the gospel to those who have never heard it before. Pray for me to have wisdom in the midst of local and provincial government persecution.

"Our God is higher than any authority."

Reigning in Life – Pastor Wu

Life as a child in my small village in China was very rewarding. My parents taught me from the Bible, and as a young boy, I would cry tears of joy whenever I could go to church. I grew up in our family house church where my father preached.

My love for the peasants has always been very strong. Often I would join with other believers in helping to build someone's house or in bringing food to a poor farmer who had almost no possessions. I had no idea God was grooming me to later serve Him or how all those small efforts would result in events that have the potential to create *global changes*.

During one season, our house church began to multiply a hundred times. We would often have gatherings of two thousand believers. This was significant for a rural area. However, a day came when the local authorities began to monitor our activities very carefully. The government officials heard about a huge gathering of people who were following a western religion.

One day in 1974, the officials showed up without any warning and apprehended several leaders, including myself. They seized all the Bibles and our furniture. Most leaders were sentenced to three years in prison, but since I played such a significant role in the house church, I was sentenced to life in prison. Despite the challenges, somehow I still had boldness. I did not deny my God. Remaining faithful during adversity resulted in much personal joy.

I was badly beaten by the police because I was an influential person in that part of the country. Thousands of believers came to hear my encouraging teachings. Our ministry included healings and miracles.

In prison, I had to work hard in a labor camp for sixteen to eighteen hours every day, but the Lord was with me. He gave me peace and strength that no one in this world could take away. I got used to all the suffering because I focused on the cross that Jesus carried. Because of Him, I could smile in my heart, even when I was unjustly beaten and accused.

My prison time seemed to last forever! Winter seemed to go on year after year. During the times when I began to lose hope in the Lord, I would remember the stories of the apostle Paul that are recorded in the book of Acts.

In 1997, I was miraculously released after spending twenty-three years in prison. Outside the prison walls, I continued to choose to live for God because I wanted people to know that I was not afraid to suffer for Jesus. I thought, "Jesus suffered much more for my sins even though He was completely innocent. His death made salvation possible for all the people of the world."

Over the course of several years, the police came on six different occasions and warned me to stop holding church meetings. Each time, I was taken to prison and heavily fined. All my possessions were taken from me.

It was disappointing to return home and discover that all the Bibles and songbooks were gone. I did not have anything to sell to get money to purchase more, nor did I know anyone else who could help my body of believers.

Amazingly and thankfully, many of us had memorized a few Bible chapters; therefore, we could still encourage others to grow in the Lord! My repeated prayer was, "God forgive the authorities for they did not know what they were doing."

Later, some Americans gave us 3,000 Bibles. Now, we intently pray for their nation.

Today, the house churches I lead have several thousand believers in attendance. Their membership spans across four different provinces. This has led to regional changes and a global impact...*we are even able to reach out to Muslim nations and take the gospel into North Korea.* Each church also has set goals to send hundreds of missionaries to far-away, remote parts of China.

God is on the move!

Even So: Sister Sheng, Her Mother, and the Gospel

Trials or difficulties of any kind can lead to the temptation to give up all hope and quit. Many brothers and sisters in China face persecution daily. Yet, they hold onto hope and remain faithful to God.

One of these dear saints is Sister Sheng. She has faced more trials than she could ever count or care to remember. She first heard the gospel when she was twenty-five years old. Ever since that time, she has given her life to Christ and has served God and his people.

When God called her, she began working with poor immigrant workers in the province of Sichuan. As she obeyed the calling on her life and God's instructions, God blessed her and gave her favor with the people. She was able to minister to many people. Her ministry produced fruitful results. Just like what happened in the New Testament book of Acts, many were healed and added to the church.

However, she was scorned by some of the locals and then persecution came. Once, she was taken captive. She was then threatened and warned not to help others or share Christ with them.

Sheng refused to submit to the threats. She was not afraid of her captors. She believed the promise in Romans 8:31, and declared, "If God is for me, who can be against me?" She knows God will protect her. She does not worry about her life or her safety but continues to share the love of Christ with those who want to hear.

Sister Sheng works within several provinces. She has faced many trials as her ministry grows. In Yunnan province, she was falsely accused for being involved with drugs. After being convicted, she was sent to prison for nearly five years. The conditions within the prison were not good. She shared her cell with thirty other people who were drug dealers and addicts. Most nights were full of interruptions and chaos and she went without sleep. On the first night, her bed sheet was stolen by a bigger inmate.

In addition to her lack of sleep, she was deprived of food as well. She was always bullied into "sharing" what little she had. Despite the harsh environment, Sister Sheng did not focus on how bad her situation was. Rather, she took every concern she had to God. As she prayed for mercy and strength, God was always faithful to give her enough strength for each new day.

Sister Sheng's trials did not always come from outside sources; she also faced health problems. While in prison, Sheng had a persistent fever and began to lose weight quickly. The doctors tried giving her various kinds of medicine but nothing worked. Sheng continued to pray for God's mercy and healing.

After a month, her fever finally broke. However, the good news was short lived when the doctors found a tumor, the size of a large egg, growing in her stomach. Sadly, Sheng was diagnosed with cancer.

When her mother heard the news, she worked long hours to find a way to help her daughter. She visited her in prison and attempted to get special permission from the government to take Sheng to a reputable hospital.

When her mother arrived, she was horrified when she saw how much weight her daughter had lost. She was skin and bones and barely breathing. Her health was so poor that one doctor honestly told her mother that if Sheng was taken by bus and not the train to the hospital, she would surely die…*making their efforts in vain.*

Her mother made a choice not to give in to her worst fears. She simply declared, "We believe in Jesus and I believe God will heal my child."

The doctor began to mock her, not believing that God was even real.

He angrily told Sheng's mother, "Go and ask your Jesus to save your daughter then!"

Chapter 3: Missions Leaders

Sister Sheng and her mother did not lose hope but kept praying and believing that God would make a way for her to be healed.

When the fellow brothers and sisters in Christ decided to join in prayer for Sister Sheng, the healing immediately and simply happened. She was then able to attend church regularly. She loved worshipping the Lord and through her praise, and God restored her joy and strength. She began to see God's own hand as the Lord lovingly healed her from all her health problems.

Sister Sheng's obedience to God was blessed and she continued to thrive in ministry. Then she experienced extreme favor. Her false accusers came to her and asked for her forgiveness. "My daughter's healing and freedom is nothing less than a miracle," exclaimed Sheng's mother.

Sister Sheng was later again arrested and convicted for being an unregistered and free Christian. Sheng immediately began fasting and praying. After serving one year's sentence, she was finally released in the province of Sichuan.

She now remains under the government's surveillance, but she continues to worship as a Christian and will do what she calls, "taking care of God's Kingdom business." Although the authorities keep watch over her, she does not stray from or compromise the gospel. Because of Sister Sheng's faithfulness and trust in God, the province of Sichuan is home to the centers where 1,200 leaders are trained every three years. These leaders are taught the Word of God and equipped to serve and bring the gospel to those who have not heard it before.

Hundreds of leaders are sent into remote villages to do kingdom ministry work. Sister Sheng has a plan and a vision. She wants to plant over 100 churches all over Northeast China.

Please join me in prayer that Sister Sheng will accomplish her goals and continue in her calling.

Chapter 4: Nations Need You

It is difficult to determine how China has influenced Christianity in Tibet. As an independent state, the Dalai Lama ruled Tibet, and Buddhism was the state religion. Then in 1951, Mao Dedong's forces invaded Tibet, viciously demolishing the centuries-old Lamaist political system, the physical Buddhist stronghold, and annexing the country as a nominally autonomous territory of the People's Republic of China. The Chinese attacked monasteries and killed monks until the end of the Cultural Revolution (1966-1967). They put down a revolt in 1959 by massacring thousands of Tibetans, forcing the Dalai Lama and 100,000 of his supporters to flee to India. Many Buddhists today who demonstrate for Tibetan independence flee for their lives into Nepal, Bhutan, or India. In the midst of all this terror, one wonders if the Tibetans questioned the ability of the Dalai Lama to save them.

The communists have softened up a bit on devotees of Buddha in recent years, allowing some monasteries to be renovated and people to worship (under watchful communist eyes). With the translation of Mao's works into Tibetan and the introduction of communist doctrine into schools, however, there is a core of people who no longer worship the Lama, as their fathers did. Some Tibetans have even joined the communist party, adopting Chinese dress and eating Chinese food. As in China, some of the people may be disillusioned and their hearts may be more open to the gospel.

While the Dalai Lama was granted political asylum in India, his religion continued to flourish in Tibet. Because of this, millions of people never heard the gospel. Spiritually, these people were living in complete and utter darkness.

For example, the Amdo group was animists who worshipped snakes, birds, and trees. Early in my missionary calling, I began to have a strong passion for the unreached Tibetan nation. Much like North Korea today, the Tibetans felt persecuted, lonely, and left out of worldwide affairs.

My brothers and I were among the first of a very few missionaries to visit Tibet during that period. We all felt the nations needed us to proclaim the good news of Jesus Christ. Similarly to how I felt about Tibet, today I have a burden to help North Koreans in the twenty-first century.

The most exciting development is that China opened Tibetan borders to travelers in 1986, providing a miraculous opportunity for Christians to enter the country as tourists. As a Restricted-Access Nation ("RAN"), Tibet's openness to outsiders is erratic and unpredictable. However, Christians can enter the country now with greater freedom than ever before.

Still, Christians do not have freedom to witness or worship. Although there are no written laws against holding a Christian meeting in public or preaching the gospel, those caught participating in those activities are almost always arrested and might be imprisoned. Foreign visitors can go only where a professional tour leads them. All Christian work, whether done by foreign visitors or the natives themselves, is strictly under cover. (16-20)

Serving Christ in Tibet (1980s): *Neil's Testimony Continued...*

Workers from The Sowers Ministry (TSM) saw that the Tibetans are open to the gospel of Jesus. When Tibet opened its borders, TSM workers visited the country to assess the situation, to explore ministry possibilities, and to feel the heartbeat of the people. In 1988 and 1989, TSM workers traveled to Lhasa and visited the Potala, Sera, Jokhang, and Drepung monasteries. As they distributed Christian literature,

Chapter 4: Nations Need You 41

Buddhist worshippers argued with each other in an attempt to get a copy, and lamas requested Bibles. They saw a genuine spiritual hunger for the Truth. The monks and lamas were fully aware that this was not another printed matter about their god-king, the Dalai Lama. Instead, many of them recognized that the books were about Jesus. It was such a blessed time to be able to place in the hands of these people a means by which the Holy Spirit can work in their lives.

In July, 1990, God provided opportunities for me to minister in Tibetan monastaries from Nepal side to Potala palace. I traveled via a road the Chinese built for security reasons.

When I arrived in Lhasa, Tibet, a two-hour drive from the airport, all I saw was green uniformed, military police everywhere. Security has been very tight in Tibet since the Beijing Massacre of June 1989.

The Lord opened the doors for me to give away Bible tracts and Gospels of John. First day, the Tibetans invited me for yak tea. On the first day I gave away fifty percent of the Christian literature. The next day, one Tibetan family invited me and a Japanese team into their home. Many monks and lamas received the literature, often reading it immediately. At the Jokhang monastery, I gave some literature to a monk and his young trainee. In such ways the Lord provided opportunities to spread the gospel. Some opened their hearts and prayed to receive Christ.

As one TSM worker says, "I am confident that slowly but surely the Lord is raising up a host of armies in that forbidden land. I have settled in my heart to pray for them regularly and visit my dear brothers as often as possible."

Tibetan Buddhism has invaded the West. Tibetan Buddhism, with its eastern mystique, appeals to intellectuals and seekers, many of whom have rejected Christianity. Resident lamas and their disciples have established Tibetan study centers in the western world. In the United States, several major universities, including Harvard, Berkeley, and Wisconsin, have set up departments of Tibetan studies. In some classes, parts of Tibetan scripture is required reading. Some countries have Tibetan Buddhist monasteries. Here's a list of them, with the approximate number of monasteries in each (16-20):

England—28
Germany—9
Italy—17
New Zealand—3
United States—42

People admire the Dalai Lama, the spiritual leader of Tibetan Buddhists. He won the Nobel peace prize in 1989 in recognition that the beliefs of Tibetan Buddhism are of fundamental importance to the world. An advocate of ecumenism, the Lama said that belief in God "does not matter so much." To a follower of Tibetan Buddhism, Jesus is seen as the "incarnate principle of enlightenment" rather than the unique Son of God. Tibetan Buddhism does not acknowledge God the Father or His Son, Jesus. Tibetan Buddhism and Christianity do not mix. (16-20)

Often I have thoughts about Western cultures. I do not see many churches concerned about mission work, especially in the severely persecuted nations. I wonder, "Is the Western gospel a pure gospel?" I am reminded that Galatians 1:6-7 states, "I am astonished that you are so quickly deserting the one who called you to live in the grace of Christ and are turning to a different gospel which is really no gospel at all. Evidently some people are throwing you into confusion and are trying to pervert the gospel of Christ," (7). Often I question, "Are the dedicated, suffering missionaries aware of the state of the Christian church in the West?"

I have felt the calling of God to be salt and light to the best of my ability, no matter where I am (Matthew 5:13-14). Back then, I felt motivated, perhaps like John the Baptist was motivated, to give a specific message for certain people groups for God-ordained purposes.

Today I still have the same urge to proclaim that the Kingdom of God is truly at hand. I have desired to bear fruit for Christ since very early on in my life. I believe God himself birthed a desire in my heart to travel the world...even when I was a small boy I would watch the planes fly overhead and wonder when God would enable me to fly.

The following is a testimony of another man called to missions. His parents were missionaries in South America where he was raised. Now he is operating successful businesses and is dedicated to funding missionaries around the world. His dedication to the cause of Christ causes Him to know the desperate need that nations have to hear the truth from us who have already heard it multiple times.

Pray that God will raise up Christian workers to go to Tibet, and to Tibetan converts everywhere. Pray that they will see and follow God-given strategies for extending His kingdom.

Teaching by Entrepreneur M. Lewis

When I read the Word, I see it as contractual, a covenant, legal and technical. It is like reading the blueprint of a house. It is not a reference. It is specific. Jeremiah 29:11, Romans 8:28 and Proverbs are like business advice. The Word is also like looking at a different kind of math. To understand that leads to success.

I have also noticed two examples of transitions in the Bible. Joseph of Arimathea was a wealthy man. He is mentioned during the telling of when Christ was crucified. During that time, an earthquake occurred, which reminds me of an apocalyptic event. Many did not respect Jesus' body that had been crucified. This man, Joseph, did and offered his wealth *and* property. Some scholars estimate Joseph's gift could be comparable to the value of an entire house in that day.

The Bible also says it took multiple people to move the stone away that was sealing the tomb. (See Matt. 27:66.) I think this man helped people understand how important the death of Christ was. We cannot judge circumstances. Along with all the signs and wonders, this man's actions had to shake up the religious leaders.

The Romans eventually realized that they had made a mistake and the Jewish leaders could not admit they did not properly judge the time they were living in. They were in a time of transition and a process of emptying out themselves. Sometimes things get worse before they get better. Sometimes people allow circumstances to cloud an accurate view of God. I believe that just like during that period, today the world is going through transition again.

Think about the story of the children of Israel coming out of Egypt. Horrible things happened *through* the people of God and not *to* the people of God. The purpose of these catastrophic events was to transform the world. God's people exited slavery as victors and not victims. However, they constantly complained to Moses, their leader.

Three days after leaving Egypt, God's people found themselves between two mountains, so-to-speak, the Red Sea ahead of them, and Pharaohs' chariots coming behind them. Almost all of God's people judged God based on the circumstances, and they even thought that Moses might be working with the Egyptians. This reminds me of the type of paranoid thinking exhibited by Adolf Hitler.

Really, the people should have looked to their God in order to judge the circumstances correctly. Likewise, Christians should know that eventually something always has to shift because God is our Deliverer. This paranoid thinking is a recurring problem.

Even today, media and advertisements bombard us. It is said that people experience 60,000 persuasions per day! As human beings, we have to process all this information while still looking to God get directions from the Holy Spirit. Christians must learn how to apply His resources and gifts as we go through transitions.

Unique opportunities are presenting themselves to us in today's world. God is allowing certain circumstances to happen for the next generation to know where to look. We must look to Him for the good of the Kingdom. We also need to expand our vision and think about our families. Know that is it very possible that your own brothers and sisters may have the very resources that can benefit the kingdom and allow God to fulfill His destiny in your life. God gives ideas, methods, and systems for us to be victorious, and we should pursue those with all of our heart. These things could unlock nation-to-nation relationships and open doors for the gospel.

Cyrus of Myanmar

My father's prayer while I was in my mother's womb was for me to become a minister, one whom God would use for fulfilling His Great Commission. Throughout my youthful years, he continued to encourage and pray for me to clearly know my purpose and to stay focused on God.

His specific prayer was for me to spend my entire life leading and mentoring people for God. As a young adult, I decided to attend a Bible college. After I passed my matriculation, I started to be interested in and have a passion for doing Christian ministry. I do believe that God answered the prayers of my father and of my Bible college teachers in Burma. That is why I am where I am today.

The more I learn the Word of God and meditate on it, the more I love Him. The more I love Him, the more I love His people. As my love for His people increases, He enables me to become more of a servant-leader to work in the ministry of helps for people (1 Corinthians 12:27-28). This revelation has changed and continues to change my earthly mindset. I have learned that those who can inspire others to dream more, learn more, do more, love more, and become more as a great leader are great leaders themselves.

Now I oversee about fifty to seventy people in Chin state, Myanmar, including church members, church leaders, pastors, Agape children, and Bible college students.

Big problems require godly mentoring. Because of this fact, leaders must be dependent upon God. Too many people have a weakness of being too dependent on their ministers. Many believers do not read their Bible and seem to just believe everything their leaders tell them.

We must prevent this because it can lead to cultish activities. In some churches, people even consider it okay to practice witchcraft or to communicate with evil spirits. Usually these people are weary from suffering. They have not renewed their minds; therefore, they still believe evil spirits can heal them from serious diseases.

The Church is characterized by both human and godly attributes because it is the Body of Christ. Still, it is an institution of human beings. My prayer is that God will give church leaders, myself included, the wisdom necessary to handle these issues without causing resentment. I also consult with other church leaders to unite for a corporate anointing and find the best God-given way of handling these problems.

Changing His Nation by Discipleship: Sheng of Zheijiang, China

Sheng grew up in rural China. His family came from Buddhism and suffered much for their faith in Christ. He had been imprisoned four times in his early years for following Jesus Christ. Now he says that even in hard times, Jesus is his strength and joy.

Sheng has faced many struggles while pastoring and leading training sessions. Many times, he had to change his places of worship and meetings. Yet, the more persecution he faced, the more he saw great results for the expansion of God's Kingdom.

He stated, "I am sowing His Word in all the needy places; often these places are difficult to reach but the Lord gives me strength. I was able to spend much time in prayer with our leaders. We have set up centers in strategic places on the mountains where 400-600 leaders can be trained. Please pray for us as we spend more time training tribal leaders so they can go out evangelizing the lost and combating false teachers with the truth. This will make our local churches strong and full of God's power."

Some of Sheng's leaders went back and planted 180 cell churches. They now have over 21,000 believers in Henan province. His churches are growing, experiencing God's love, and are anointed to reach the lost, heal the sick, and mend the brokenhearted. Awesome is the work of our God!

After much prayer and fasting, he was able to continue meeting in different locations. There are now more than 320 believers gathering for worship in these two cities. There is rejoicing and praising with every new convert.

Sheng is changing his nation with God's power by the Holy Spirit.

Chapter 5: Taking Risks

Neil's Testimony Continued...

In order to risk everything for God, Christians cannot be too sophisticated in doing the works of the gospel. In the book of John 15, we read how fishermen were called to be disciples of Christ. As they obeyed His voice, they began to be transformed into the likeness of Christ and started to function as missionaries.

Our obedience should yield lasting results, or what the Scriptures call "fruit that remains," (John 15:16). Righteousness can then come to earth and invade darkness. As a result, the Church can be filled with God's Holy Spirit power and function without spot or wrinkle (Ephesians 5:27).

Testings in Tibet

During the 1980s, my journey to Lhasa, Tibet, I often hitchhiked along barren, dangerous roads. There was no expected time of arrival, since the vehicles I rode in frequently broke down during the long-distance commutes. Bandits raiding the buses I rode in were common occurrences. Ten to fifteen men would force the driver to stop. Then a few of them would board the bus and rob all the passengers.

Preaching in Tibet means traveling Tibetan roads and requires surrendering your life to God during the journey and during every stop the vehicles make. During the trips, I also had to endure the strong smells of the Buddhist lamas' musty blankets and the volatile gasoline fumes emitted by the bus. On a few occasions, I even got a headache and actually vomited because of the harsh conditions.

There were times when the driver would stop at small monasteries where the Tibetans would burn candles and sleep a few hours at night...*without any blankets*. All the smoke from the many burning candles would literally take my breath away. I would ask the question, "How much longer God?" That is when God reminded me of Joshua 24:15, "But if serving the LORD seems undesirable to you, then choose for yourselves this day whom you will serve..." (7).

Let me encourage you, my reader; decide today whom you will serve.

As a young believer, I obeyed God and ventured to remote and difficult places in the world where I knew villagers had never heard about or experienced Jesus. My compassion for the lost even led me to the secluded people living in high elevations and rugged terrain surrounding Mount Everest.

Riding in vehicles in this territory is still fresh in my memory. Just sitting in a truck or a bus was a painful experience. I ended up traveling to this area of the world over a dozen times. I remember the dusty roads, cheap tobacco smoke, the landslides, and the drunk drivers who were never policed.

When I would begin to doubt my calling, God would ask, "Are you willing to obey my Word and take it to this region of the world?" The conditions were almost unbearable. But the most despicable circumstances could not compare with the passionate love of the Father for lost people. My endurance, along with that of my brothers, would yield a harvest of people who began to have amazing encounters with God.

Once, a Buddhist lama confessed Jesus Christ as his Savior while on his deathbed. I was then permitted to ask God for a miracle and healing came upon him. God raised him off his deathbed.

His family had already begun the process of preparing his body to be strapped to a yak and transported to the mountaintop in order for the *jhator* to dispose of his body by feeding his remains to the vultures. This is their custom because, in that high terrain, they do not have enough pliable soil in which to bury the dead.

It was at this moment the family invited me in and asked me to pray for him! Lo and behold, he got saved *and* healed! Because of the healing power of God released through believing faith, the following day we were able to lead the whole family in deciding to follow Jesus Christ.

The prayer of Jabez gives us insights into our purpose for living here on earth, "Jabez cried out to the God of Israel, "Oh, that you would bless me and enlarge my territory! Let your hand be with me, and keep me from harm so that I will be free from pain." And God granted his request" (1 Chronicles 4:10)(7). The Bible says Jabez got what he asked for.

Prayer is simply reasoning with God by standing on His promises. Truly, if a Christian counts the cost of a mission as a worthy thing, does not fear, and simply believes God, prayers are answered.

God manifested his power that day in the remote regions of Tibet and will continue to do so for those who seek after and obey Him, regardless of where they are on this planet. Hallelujah!

Another time I traveled to Tibet with a suitcase full of Bibles and Christian literature. A tremendous miracle happened when I passed through all the Tibetan airport security without being checked.

Despite that huge victory, I arrived at my hotel and quickly hid the literature under the bed. Fearful thoughts slowly started filling my mind. The fear became so great that I almost convinced myself to throw the literature into the Yarlung River nearby. Thankfully, I did not obey my fears and the literature was delivered into the right hands.

More Motivation

Reverend Ingolf Schmid (name changed for safety reasons) originally from Poland, is the first persecuted believer that I met in 1983. His appearance is still fresh in my mind. He was wearing a green jacket, looked to be in his fifties, and, because of his unique mustache, appeared to be German.

Ingolf's parents were killed during the Second World War when Hitler was putting Jews into captivity in slave labor camps. As a result of the death of his parents, Ingolf had been raised in a refugee camp.

After the war, he was literally skin and bones and dying of sickness. Ingolf was kept in a facility by the Allies, who attempted to reunite him with his parents. Undocumented persons were subject to scrutiny because of Nazi attempts to pass themselves off as refugees. Even though his family had been destroyed in the Holocaust, and there was no one alive to be restored to, Ingolf was released from the relocation camp because of his young age.

Later on, during a summer youth camp, Ingolf gave his life to the Lord and God called him into ministry. He ended up traveling all around world. Ingolf was the first person I met who had been a prisoner. Recalling his life story helped me when I would later be jailed for doing missions work. I believe meeting him and hearing his story was part of the process of God preparing me to be strong and endure jail.

Stories of Robert Morrison of Scotland, one of the first Protestant missionaries to China, also inspired me to endure hardship. He spent twenty-seven years of his life in two provinces and translated the entire Bible into Chinese.

As years went on, more incredible missionary stories motivated me. I have learned how God used a common believer, like Sister Rong, to raise five people from the dead in the Anhui and Zheijiang

Provinces. All five of the miracle recipients became believers who remained active in the church with signs and wonders following them.

In Luke 17:21, The New Testament reveals the Kingdom of Heaven is in our midst. Over my years of serving God, I have learned it is inside of each believer. Because I heard the gospel at a young age, I recognized the presence of the Kingdom of God living in me sooner than others were able to understand.

We serve a supernatural God who desires to reveal Himself. I know this is true because I have heard Buddhist monks testify that they found Christ in their hearts as a result of having dreams. During these visitations of the Holy Spirit, several reported dreams in which they saw Buddha in hell. As a result, they were scared to continue practicing Buddhism.

Gospel means good news. The power of the gospel is manifesting and bringing the good news of revival into all situations throughout Asia.

More Defining Moments of My Faith

Once after witnessing to Himalayans tribal groups in Nepal, my brothers and I were compelled to cross the Friendship Bridge between Nepal and China. We had to pass by armed guards with guns in order to step into communist China and pray the blessings of God upon the nation. My worst fear became reality when, as a new Christian, I was apprehended. I found myself praying for God's help and wisdom...*even after being obedient to Him*. During this time, I learned an important lesson: captives may be in prison, but they can be free in their heart.

While carrying the gospel around the world, I have been apprehended several times during my missionary calling.

Several years later, God enabled me to travel to Holland. A question came to mind during that trip, "What is the gospel of good tidings to earth?" In Holland, I was never afraid while giving out good tidings. While traveling with a group of evangelists, I preached the gospel just outside a building where a large Hindu Convention had gathered. Soon after sharing, some radical Hollanders beat me.

During the beating, God reminded me of a Scripture in Matthew chapter 5, "Blessed are the peace makers."(7) The world is filled with unrest as people live in ignorance of the peace that only comes by knowing Him.

God's love is unconditional, and that is how He wants us to love others. As I continued to share the gospel, many continued to reject me and my message. Even so, Christians should never lose their passion and devotion. We are called to be lights in this dark world (Matthew 5:13-14) and to care for the less fortunate (Matthew 25:40).

Das of India

Observing the call of God and seeing the work of The Sowers Ministry compelled me to step into ministry leadership. I was touched by the Lord to humble myself and to invite others be a part of something making a huge difference in ministry in my nation of India.

In spite of hardship and facing death, leaders continue to serve the Lord. I have seen blind eyes restored to sight, the sick healed, and the dead raised because of godly leadership.

Sadly, a pastor was burned to death because of these awesome moves of God. I have found that prayer and fasting are major actions for the leaders to see miracles like in Jesus' day.

The Anderson brothers have taught me for many years, and I still continue to learn from them. I teach others principles on breakthrough in leadership. Thousands of leaders were trained by the Andersons during the last twenty-five years. I have seen huge church growth in India, Nepal, and Thailand. When leaders have loving and kind mentors, people flourish and make a solid impact in ministry and leadership.

Chapter 5: Taking Risks

Huge changes occurred in my life after accepting Christ. It gave me life lessons to share with others, including telling them about how great God is. God is constantly teaching me as I spend time with Him. I am learning each day and waiting on God to open doors to touch lives.

Because many are ignorant of this teaching, I want to do more to train leaders. Leaders must be willing to be humble and to spend quality time in seeking God each day. This allows God to speak His plans and strategies on how to do ministry effectively.

God wants to talk to us. Effective leaders keep their ears open and are obedient to His words. Quality time with God and following the Holy Spirit can accomplish mighty works for the Lord. We do not have to be afraid of wicked men who want to kill or poison us or our families. I am convinced that even though there are people who want to harm the work of the ministry, all we need is more of the Lord.

A great leader is humble and faithful to the Lord. At times, it is hard to be a leader, to teach or break ground in hard places among Christians or certain mindsets. Leaders pray, lead, guide and visit the sick. Leaders love to be around believers and people in general.

I shepherd about forty or fifty leaders in India. At the same time, I am mentoring and learning how to be humble. We all must carry our own cross each day.

I manage problems through prayer and fast regularly. I want to be like Jesus by loving people and hating sin. There must be an honest way to manage problems.

Persecuted Pastor Lee

Pastor Lee was born into a Christian family in China. His parents were leaders at one of the local underground churches. As the Cultural Revolution progressed, there was an increase in persecution toward the church and its members. Three men from Lee's congregation were taken into custody. The government threatened to not only destroy the church, but also terminate its leaders; thus, Lee's parents were at risk.

By God's grace, nothing worse happened. As time passed, the situation began to look better and peace returned to the Christian community. Lee reached the point where he strived to dedicate his life and heart to the Lord. Such change came to Lee's life that he shifted his goals from studying politics and the law to attending Bible school where he dedicated himself to theology and knowledge of the Word of God. He has since completed his studies and started his own ministry, which has grown immensely and exhibited great order and influence.

Pastor Lee was visited by a government leader whose wife was sick to the point of death. Instead of going to a nearby hospital, the government leader traveled from far away because he had heard about the healing power of God and wanted his wife to receive it. Pastor Lee prayed for her healing, and she was miraculously healed.

The healing of the prominent lady was such a miracle that it caused large crowds of people to visit the church. Lee told the people that he had healed no one. The miracle was the Lord's mighty work and Jesus alone deserved the glory for it.

Pastor Lee then decided to move toward a mountainous area and expand his prayer ministry. As a result, many nonbelievers heard the gospel and received the Word of God for the first time.

In 1983, Pastor Lee and several of his fellow leaders were arrested by the police and imprisoned for several weeks. During the time they were jailed, their ministry facilities were destroyed by explosives that had been placed there by the police.

During this same time, Lee was questioned concerning his church. When he would not give the investigators all the information they wanted, Pastor Lee was hung upside down for sixty hours. While this was taking place, his congregation back on the mountain fervently prayed for his protection and release. The Lord came through and delivered Pastor Lee.

Pastor Lee was released a few weeks later. He continues in the work of God and has been pastoring his church for more than forty years. The mother church has birthed 210 daughter churches with a total attendance of 800,000 believers. Pastor Lee is still busily involved in training young leaders to plant churches. He reports an increase in fasting and prayer in spite of the persecution in rural church settings.

Deep in the mountains, a huge revival is taking place. Thank God for ministries such as The Sowers who believe the message of God's love and mercy should be shared throughout – *even in the deepest hills and forests of China.*

Strong churches need qualified leaders who know how to pray and preach the gospel that causes correct order and influences others. May God continue to bless Sowers as they take the gospel of Jesus Christ to those who desperately need to hear it.

Unstoppable Wong

Pastor Wong is training gospel workers in many parts of China. He gave his life to Christ after experiencing a healing miracle in his body in 1981. Wong travels with his family to conduct leadership trainings in house churches. He also runs a secret, short-term training center in the remote mountains for 180 people, and pastors several other fast-growing churches. Thousands of believers meet in his house churches.

As a pastor from Taiwan was teaching leaders, the police came and interrupted the meetings. As a result, Wong spent three months in prison and was fined 4,000 RMB ($800 USD). This did not deter his activities though, and he continued to travel to remote areas of China.

Pastor Wong personally baptized over 2,000 new believers, discipled 3,000 young leaders, and planted 65 churches within the past two years. He and his coworkers often work under the threat of arrest.

His co-workers have been put in prison for preaching the gospel and sending Bibles and teaching tapes to house church leaders. In spite of persecution, the local believers meet in homes, factories, and even forests.

Wong's ministry is full of miracle stories of God's protection, provision, healing, and answers to problems. Once, he baptized a woman who had muscular problems in both arms and was not able to move them. As she went under the water, she was touched by the power of God. She came out of the water completely healed and received full movement of her arms. All pain was gone. Seeing this miracle of healing, her whole family became Christians and started attending church.

Pastor Wong always urges his church members to evangelize the lost. He himself travels extensively as an evangelist and teacher in the northeastern parts of China. In one province, he stays busy overseeing twenty-four new churches with over 4,000 believers. When asked about his passion in the ministry, his response was, "I train up new workers to harvest the souls." He provides hands-on training projects for young gospel workers.

Professor Bi of China

Professor Bi (Mr. B) was born in China in 1937 and has had many uncommon experiences throughout his lifetime. During his childhood education, he spent one year in a Catholic middle school. After high school, he attended Beijing University and graduated with a B.S. Degree in Mathematics. Following his college education, Bi spent eleven years in the Chinese Air Force as an aerodynamics teacher.

At the age of thirty, and as a member of the intellectual class, he was imprisoned and endured eighteen months of torture and hard labor under the Red Guards because of his profession. This is when Bi experienced "re-education" during China's Cultural Revolution.

Professor Bi witnessed his close friends shot to death after refusing to wear a Red Guard badge. This grieved Bi greatly, but after one year of suffering, he decided to end his life by jumping from the third floor window of the building where he was imprisoned. However, God supernaturally intervened and called him to salvation and to service for His kingdom.

By God's grace, six months later, he was released from prison and began Christian ministry. He learned from Jesus' examples in the Bible, forgave everyone, and pursued a Christ-like life.

For almost five decades, Bi has lived his life goal of being a burden bearer for his Lord. Still true to his initial desire to train up an army of leaders that would change China for the kingdom of God, Professor Bi has faithfully served the Body of Christ in every manner possible at every opportunity available to him.

Now, as a retired professor of physics, he works as a full-time missionary for Jesus Christ. His busy life includes taking care of many house churches, preaching, coordinating the distribution of Christian materials in China, helping handicapped schoolchildren and street children, helping laid-off and "waiting for work" Chinese Christians, and working with China's orphanages.

Recently, he found out from his father that his family has a Jewish heritage. This explained why he was led to establish a residence in a Jewish community and minister to the Chinese Jews there. In 1999, he was the representative of China's Jews at the Feast of Tabernacles celebration in Jerusalem.

As time permits, he translates Christian materials from English to Chinese and arranges for them to be printed for distribution to believers all over China. Churches are growing rapidly in China, and Bi is sold out to growing them God's way. He has ministered in many churches and trained countless leaders for the growth of the house church movement. Because of Bi's obedience, millions of believers are now ready to face the challenges of being a Spirit-filled Christian in a communist nation.

Believers are not afraid to stand up for freedom and righteousness. Bi will continue to bear burdens for Christ, share his experiences in order to promote the gospel in China, and help in raising up godly leaders to assist his brothers and sisters in China.

Lamuel of India

Pastor Lamuel was born in a Hindu family that lived in a very high-caste Brahman society. These castes are the only people who can do puja, a specific form of idol worship and offer sacrifices to Hindu gods. His father was very much involved in these rituals.

Before his birth, his mother became frustrated when life seemed to get even harder after worshiping idols. She looked up to heaven and prayed that the One True God would give her a better life. During this time, many witch doctors were killing newborns as offerings to gods. His mother prayed and fasted several days in order to reroute demons. Lamuel's mother did not know if she would have to encounter witch doctors. But during the night, two angels came and reassured her that everything would be okay. The angels said, "We will save your newborn." Because of these events, Lamuel's mother dedicated him to God when he was in her womb.

While inside a church at the age of twelve, Lamuel gave his life to the Lord. He then began to learn the Bible and sincerely pray. At age seventeen, Lamuel went to a Bible school and learned to serve in ministry. Then at the age of twenty-one, he immersed himself in a lifestyle of prayer, became a full-time gospel worker for the church, and has been serving the Lord as a pastor ever since. He currently oversees twenty churches. No, it has not been easy being a pastor in India where persecution is sometimes common. In recent years, many of his own converts have been kidnapped and beaten. Pastor Lamuel himself has been persecuted.

Once, huge persecution broke out in his area and over 195 churches were burned. Many believers were killed or burned alive.

Another time, Hindu radicals came and separated thirty-five believers just prior to their being baptized. They shouted at him and said they would kill him and his family. These threats, while common, must be taken seriously and fought with prayer and fasting.

Later, while he was sharing the Word with seventy new believers in a village, a crowd came and wanted to kill the pastors. Pastor S. Mallik was bound by these radical Hindu people. Pastor Mallik was from Adivasi group (an untouchable, low society caste). He was commanded to deny Jesus in order to live. Pastor Mallik refused to deny Jesus as his Lord and Savior. The radicals then cut one of his hands open. While he was bleeding, they commanded him once more to deny Jesus and forget church work. The Hindus promised to let him live if he would renounce his faith. Pastor Mallik replied, "I have served Him for thirty years and He has been faithful to me. How can I deny Him now?" The radicals then proceeded to kill Pastor Mallik and his family.

Despite the risks involved, Lamuel, his wife and their two daughters (ages nineteen and eleven) decided to follow and serve Jesus. He is now forty-six years old, and he testifies that he will continue to serve God for many more years along with his family.

On occasion, Hindu crowds come and destroy all of the Christians' property. Nothing is left. Women are raped and pastors are burned. Children become orphaned. As a result, many believers have no place to stay and are forced to live under tents. The majority of Bibles in the Oriya and Kui languages have been burned.

Pastor Lamuel's vision is to evangelize and give Bibles to new believers while demonstrating the strong prayer life that is necessary to

Christian living. He is baptizing new saints in his surrounding areas. Many children are also in need of schooling and homes to live in. They need the Word of God, food, clothes and shelter.

Pastor Lamuel provides these things as financial support comes in. His desire is to continue to preach and teach the Word. Instead of becoming discouraged when severe persecution arises, Pastor Lamuel's heart gets full of the fire of God. He and his workers fast and pray faithfully each week. He testifies, "God is with us as we spread His Word. Please pray for us and the church family. May the Lord give us His power to go on and praise Him. Matthew 5 says, 'Blessed are those who hunger and thirst for righteousness.'" (7)

More from Lamuel/Missionary Leader Testimony

When I was seventeen years old, the Lord called me into ministry. After finishing my theological training, the Lord led me to a specific location to engage in ministry. My first mentor was my pastor, P.S. Samuel. He guided me in the ministry. Dr. George Chavanil Kamanil was a leader who also guided me and led me to do ministry.

For years, I worked hard and did not care about my health because I was so concerned for other Christians. Uncle George and the Rev. Dr. Neil Anderson mentored me in the areas of taking care of my physical needs and providing for my family. They taught me to follow God with a great heart and to be an example as a leader. The training I received at The Haggai Institute changed my mindset in order to take even better care of my family.

Another area that increased was my knowledge regarding finances. The Lord taught me by experience that I don't need to be worried about financing His work. He provides according to His own ability (Philippians 4:19). Ministry belongs to Him. I must work under Him and for Him.

A faithful life is necessary. Godly character is required for ministry.

Humility is one of the measuring rods of ministry. A leader must be humble, full of integrity, and trust in the Lord. A lifestyle of prayer and fasting is necessary to living in victory. Each week, we fast and pray for our gospel work, churches, and families. This is the reason our churches are growing so fast.

Yes, I have been heavily persecuted and even beaten by many people who do not yet know Christ. I have learned to forgive and pray for them. Instead of remaining bitter, I visit their families, give gifts, and educate their children.

Thousands of churches are experiencing healing and increasing in numbers. We are now transitioning young leaders to move into leadership positions within our churches.

At present, I mentor thirty-nine leaders in our church. Our daughter churches consist of more than fifty leaders whom I also mentor. This year, I plan to have more than 120 people receiving Christian mentoring.

I take my problems to the Lord in prayer and fasting, but I also share them with my praying friends who minister wisdom and suggestions into my life. My ministerial work is done according to the guidance of the Holy Spirit. I also seek the suggestions of elders within the church.

The senior pastor of our mission, who works under five other ministers, commissioned me. These leaders are very much committed to the call of God and to leadership. They are busily leading over 400 churches and schools. They have taught me how to take the lead and perform with the qualities of a leader. God's ways are the best and absolutely necessary in forming a solid foundation.

Honesty and humility are important in the life of a leader. Allowing others to exercise their strengths is necessary for unlocking the leader within them

My mentor is Rev. Nallaiah Aaron, the founder of Zion Pentecostal Church. Even though he has fasted and prayed, he has suffered a lot of hardship due to persecution from his family. When a person converts to Christianity from a different religion, it can be very hard to follow God. That person is often forced to leave behind their family and friends. But with prayer, God intervenes in the situation and helps.

As a leader and pastor, my burden for lost souls has increased. Many are beaten when they stand up for their love for Jesus. They choose to leave everything and follow Jesus. Why? They unlock the leader inside by denying themselves as Jesus denied Himself when He suffered and died for us. We teach these leaders to fast and pray in order to seek God and His help. We must be Jesus-minded leaders who exhibit love, care, faith, and, when needed, long-suffering.

The Bible reveals Moses as a great leader. I desire to be like Moses. In my weaknesses, I desire for God to help me as He helped Moses.

Leaders in India have many problems because they are surrounded by idol worship and Jesus haters. Believers are known to have been killed just for raising his/her voice in a heart-felt song about Jesus. As a leader, I want to share how His Holy Spirit and power can help build the Church.

Our churches are similar to New Testament churches in that we see a demonstration of power, the release of anointing and miracles. We are experiencing an annual growth rate of 5 percent in Indian churches. We encourage leaders to live godly and prayerful lives.

During this time of my life, I mentor over thirty pastors and leaders in India. During the last several years, Hindus have come at night and destroyed our property, which we use for gospel crusades. As we have prayed, fasted, and bound enemy forces, we have seen the Lord sharpen our leadership skills and open more doors. I know the Holy Spirit will help me mentor hundreds of people in the years to come as I continue in humility and live sacrificially.

Chapter 5: Taking Risks

When I face problems, I pray and speak the Word of God over the situation. When Jesus had a problem or faced loneliness, He prayed to the Father and gained strength and joy. Jesus always asked for help. In the same way, I like to pray away my problems. I seek His will and wisdom concerning every difficulty I face.

A Modern Day Apostle Paul, Li Wai

Growing up in a dangerous place like the Laoliang Province in China taught Li Wai at a young age that he must take risks in order to survive. Under his father's control and influence, Li learned the world was a harsh place. He was conditioned to know the world will always steal from and use you. It will dictate how much you can have and even what to do with what you own.

In order to be successful, Li believed one had to get revenge and push back even harder. He learned to persecute others in order to succeed in life. His father's teachings and advice promoted alcohol, drugs, and violence. His father planned to mentor Li to be a gang leader and called this a dream that Li's grandfather would be proud of.

At eight years old, Li's initiation began. He was taught Kung Fu with the reasoning that he would be better able to defend himself. He seemed to be naturally good at fighting and started to acquire a good reputation among gangsters. He was so skilled in fighting that he was feared by the people and was never met by one opponent alone. The opposition always came in numbers to challenge him. When he was ten, Li's father taught him knife-fighting techniques.

Afterward, even at such a tender age, Li began to kill people in knife fights. As a result, he became even more popular among his underworld friends. He was respected. He was feared.

Soon after Li joined a particular gang, the leader noticed his unusual fighting ability. The leader quickly recognized what an asset Li was to his group and kept Li close to him at all times.

With Li as his right-hand man, the leader was fearless. However, differences arose within the gang, and Li did not stay with the group. Thus, his father's hopes and dream of his son becoming a gang leader were crushed and never achieved. Li decided to leave his home town.

Li did heed one piece of advice his father gave him. He married a local girl and hoped for a fresh start in life.

Married life at the age of twenty was far from blissful. In fact, life became harder for Li. He was wanted by the authorities for criminal charges in relation to his past gang activities.

The young couple fled from their village to hide from the police. For the first time, the once-fearless fighter was afraid. This time his actions affected his wife and newborn baby.

Wanting to live a decent life with his family, Li was willing to do whatever it took to keep his family safe. In desperation, he cried out to God saying, "If you are real, please save me."

When he was thirty, Li met a strange man at a train station in Shenyang. This man was filled with the Holy Spirit and shared the gospel with Li.

Li listened as the man told him about the One True God and the sacrificial death of His Son, Jesus Christ, on the cross. By the revelation power of the Holy Spirit, the man also began to speak to him about facts that only Li knew.

This man somehow seemed to know Li's past deeds. He told him boldly that he was … "a wicked man hiding from the police." The man did not condemn Li, but instead encouraged him by sharing with him a message of hope, "Jesus loves you, Li."

He continued, "If you believe in Jesus, God will protect you, love you, and give you peace."

To Li, this overwhelmingly amazing news sounded too good to be true, but Li decided to trust God. He gave his life over to Jesus and began to seek His direction.

Chapter 5: Taking Risks

In the years that followed, Li was mentored by Christian leaders...*one being his mother-in-law*. He also made a deliberate decision to attend church. His first visit was unforgettable.

The moment he entered the sanctuary, Li had an encounter with God that changed his life forever. The Holy Spirit came down upon him and he felt the presence of God to the point that he could not stand. He spent the entire service sitting and kneeling, worshipping the Lord. He knew that he could not go back to his old life. He was also convicted that he had to live a life that would influence others with the love of Christ.

Li was changed from the inside out. He received a desire and vision for ministry. Suddenly he wanted to bring many into the Kingdom of God.

Li's Apostle Paul-like encounter with God resulted in him diligently working in ministry year after year. Under the guidance and leadership of Pastor Tian, Li works with the churches in Shenyang and surrounding areas. His work in Northeast China has led to more than 28,000 converts!

The churches in the region continue to grow, and Li has a vision for the churches to grow even more. His heart's desire is to train more leaders by helping them move into spiritual growth and maturity. His prayer is that these leaders would seek out even more leaders.

Extreme needs still exist in Shenyang. Li is taking a risk to carry the gospel by fighting against the Eastern Lightning cultic group in his area.

He believes that new Christians should have their own Bibles. They need the input of the Word of God in order to be able to stand strong by using the truth of the gospel. By spending time immersed in the Word of God, Li believes the new converts are more readily able to receive and understand new revelations the Holy Spirit shows them.

Please be in prayer for Li as he continues the Lord's work.

PHOTOS

Neil as a shy, teenage boy in India.

Neil speaking on leadership training in Khabarovsk, Russia.

Leaders receiving training in Northern China.

International Day of Persecution in Washington, D.C.

Increasing awareness about religious persecution -Washington, D.C.

Open air gospel meeting in A.P. India.

Hundreds of leaders gather together for training in India.

Television broadcast with Ray Goodrich, NY.

Speaking to North Korean students.

As a believer, I always kept and still keep the world map within my view to inspire and expand my vision and to pray over nations. It is faintly visible behind me here in this picture.

25th Anniversary Missions Banquet, NY.

Neil speaking to leaders from Russia and Central Asia in Saint Petersburg.

Leadership gathering in Nepal where
there is a spiritual awakening.

Prof. Du interpreting teaching from Neil in China.
In spite of persecution, churches are on the rise.

Dr. Anderson speaking at
Global Missions Conference, NY.

Neil teaching a seminar to 400
pastors in Northern China.

Missions conference in Germany. Many German churches are very focused on mission work worldwide.

Six month Bible school in Russia where many are responding and desire to lead.

Pastors conference in Vijayawada, South India.

Largest revival with leadership training in high demand when people came from six different provinces. Some traveled a two-day journey.

Neil speaking in Houston, Texas.

Secret Christian meeting in China.
Over the last thirty years, revival and
church growth continues.

Chapter 6: Leadership & Agents of God

How do we train and appoint people? Jesus demonstrated this in the Scriptures.

Delegate! Why? We know that one person cannot do all the work alone.

Our body, like the Body of Christ mentioned in Scripture, has many parts and each has its own function. In Ephesians 4:11, Jesus appointed people to demonstrate different skills. He appointed them "To equip his people for works of service, so that the body" of believers may be built up according to Ephesians 4:12. (7)

Please note that Jesus gave these skills to enable a *group* of people to do the work. He never planned for one person to do all the work. Therefore, we as leaders follow Jesus' example and appoint people around us to do tasks according to the gifts given to them by God. This will free us to live a balanced life and ensure that ministry is being conducted by people who have the necessary skills to do so.

Success Steps

1) **Draw up a Plan.**

Leaders are the force behind any vision that is being presented to people. If a leader does not have a plan to lead their people, then that leader has planned to fail. Leaders write goals. Leaders may have many good ideas, but if they don't plan well enough, the job will never get done in the way that they envisioned it to. Take time to plan ahead! Planning involves partnership with God. Prayer is a required step. Planning involves other people, the leader completing plans, and may require the purposeful neglect of some things in order to accomplish other things. This process requires leaders to follow God and His timing.

A vision involves the question: "What changes do I need to make today to achieve goals tomorrow?" This takes your vision from an idea to an action plan.

2) **Determine What Tasks are Necessary to Complete the Plan.**
Leaders prepare and work hard. Don't be a leader who takes shortcuts and does things that are dishonest or illegal. Pray and plan. Let the wisdom you seek and need come from God. Think through every detail. Ask God to reveal what needs to be done. Your dependence on God should be genuine.

Seek God for direction and council. Advice is readily available, but make sure the counsel you receive is of God. Human wisdom can fail, but God's counsel is pure, true, and lasting. Know what God has called you to do and do not bend to other people's pressures and opinions. Be obedient to God and what He has told you to do.

3) **Find Committed Individuals.**
Leaders want all their team members to move in the same direction. They take great pride when they see that the skills of each individual are being used and then improved upon. Leaders know how to communicate their plan to cast the whole vision to the people. They know how to think and act strategically. Their efforts are focused on the group by focusing on the individual development of each team member. Identify with the members of your team. Delegating will unleash leadership potential by equipping others to lead as well. Guide and educate your leaders, as well as trust and train them. Most of all, instill your passion into your team members.

A leader balances his options and gets people involved. He knows whom he leads, communicates clearly to them, and refocuses and reminds them of the vision. Leaders engage in the task at hand by making sure their team members know the needs of the society they are targeting. They are people who know what is happening and can act decisively. True leaders are aware of what is happening and then do something about it.

On a successful team, delegation is a key learning experience for future leaders. It demonstrates that not everything can be done by one person, and shows each individual what it takes to create a team. A leader who has been part of a good team will be able to build good teams because they know what they look and feel like. A good team will function as a single organism. Not only do members work together toward a common goal, but they complement and support one another so that their work seems effortless. It is a shared passion toward the accomplishment of a shared vision. Team members need to learn to work together as a unit, and be committed to the idea of working together as a team. They may already share a vision, and have ideas about how to realize it. (Making a vision come to pass takes cooperation and patience.)

Greatness starts with wonderful people. Those who see things differently: have a knack for finding important problems, have skills in problem solving, can identify connections, and have broad interests and have experience. Every great group has a strong leader. Leaders are realistic and have attainable visions. It is a leader who can recognize and select excellence in others, as coordinators of volunteer associations who handle projects, or as managers who understand the work and what it takes to produce it.

Building a good team involves a great deal more than simply choosing members. It takes developing and communicating a vision, planning the team's mission to match the vision, and then working out how people will function together. Start with the best people you can find. No team is better than its members, and finding the best people for the job at hand is tremendously important. "Best" does not always simply mean someone who can do the work better than anyone else. It may make more sense to choose someone who's only second best at the work, but better at being a member of the team. Team members must connect on a number of levels. Look for team members committed to the team's guiding vision and those that have the passion needed.

4) **Constantly Examine the Progress of the Plan.**
Challenges will cause you to grow. They serve as food for self-motivation. Every leader will be challenged every now and then – it is healthy and essential to growth. Recognize limitations and set realistic goals, take risks, set deadlines, and then hold yourself to them. A leader should be willing to do everything he expects his team members to do. Every leader must stop and evaluate his/her progress. Evaluate every three months and make personal adjustments.

Leaders fine-tune the vision over and over – this is an important element of team building.

Whenever we teach or train others, we are appointing them to the work of the Lord. When you lead somebody to the Lord, you exhort them to become part of the Body of Christ. These individuals must understand their role in fulfilling what is known as The Great Commission to reach the lost (Matthew 28:19-20).

Training is an important part of leadership. How can you expect converts to be good leaders if they have nobody to train them? This is also why God gave us The Ultimate Trainer and Great Counselor, the Holy Spirit. In Asia and Europe, I have been teaching these principles for more than twenty years. Teaching people how the Holy Spirit guides, and seeing the results in signs, wonders, and miracles helps missionaries as they see God move in their own lives as He did in the book of Acts.

Developing Others

1) **Fuel Their Desire.**

Real leaders acknowledge the Lord and those around them. They lead their team in unity and take great pride in accomplishments and skills of each individual are used and improved. Leaders inspire people to become better and to improve their daily lives. They help others get fresh inspiration and drive to do what they are passionate about. Leaders are socially skilled motivate others to be good communicators of the vision that drives them.

2) **Impart Vision.**

Leaders reprogram their thinking in order to focus in the right direction. Leaders need to have a vision, have humility, improve communication, be energetic, and spread that energy around, as well as demonstrate authority and awareness. Leaders are taught to be motivated and in turn motivate others. Leaders meet the needs of other people. A leader must have godly attitudes, be involved in world evangelism, and know how to set goals to achieve a vision. Every leader has a responsibility to advance the gospel. Annually, thousands of leaders have been trained at our TSM missions training centers. Simple-minded people are coming to be trained to then go back and make changes in their own nations.

Without clear direction and vision, a leader is doomed to fail. A visionary is someone who presents a challenge and then is able to bring out the best in people. Leaders also make sense of purpose, strive to fulfill their goals, seek out the higher purpose, and their eyes are always on the horizon. Leaders are mentors. A leader must develop a plan, describe the purpose, impart motivational power, and trust God.

Share your vision with others. Your vision should inspire others to keep moving forward. A real vision requires knowing what changes to make today so goals can be achieved tomorrow. This turns your vision from mere talk to action.

3) **Leadership Development.**
Never discuss problems with someone who cannot solve it, because this will only burden that other person. Accountability is a big part of being a good leader. We must confide in, protect, cherish, and celebrate mentors. Teach leaders about living an ordered and disciplined life.

Failure does not frighten leaders. Trust the Lord in every season (Habakkuk 3:17). Leaders plan ahead and have personal goals for their ministry. Growth and purpose are two valuable fruit of any good leader. These create movement and momentum. As a leader, I want to encourage others to be well equipped and fall in love with leading each and every day.

A leader always pursues the best leadership skills so that they can pass them on to others. They continue to develop their leadership skills and excel in serving others. Leaders who are weak communicators can learn how to be effective in that area. Leaders sharpen character by demonstrating traits like love, compassion, humility, self-control, and a sense of balanced authority (Fruit of the Spirit – Galatians 5:22).

Chapter 6: Leadership & Agents of God

I believe even the smallest of visions can have a profound influence in the Kingdom of God. Leaders are always improving. Because things are always changing around them, a leader constantly changes as well. Leaders communicate change so that team members can refocus on the vision come to pass.

Make it a point to step back and be renewed spiritually. Integrity is an important part of leadership and depends on refreshing times. Just as you expect your followers to do things with respect and integrity, you too can be transparent in everything you do, without having to hide. Seek to do well and evaluate your daily decisions.

People may ask, "Where do I get a vision?" The answer is that visions arise, often without being sought, when we apply ourselves to study the Word of God. Then skills are obtained to carry out their profession or ministry. A leader can excel in his/her leadership ability through prayer, systematic Bible study, memorizing Scriptures, "doing" the Word of God, fellowship, witnessing to others, and through worshipping God.

4) See that Commitment and Focus Remain Strong.
Leaders believe in change, as well as in seeing the big picture. They think and act strategically, knowing that success benefits not only them but their entire team. Leaders know how to emphasize and concentrate on people's strengths, not their weaknesses. They know how to bring out the good in each person. At appointed times, stop and evaluate the individual and each team members' progress.

Leaders constantly develop their skills, which are task-related, people-related, and communication-related. Three necessary things are gaining information, developing practical skills, and growing in wisdom. Regarding a leader's physical health, breathing, healthy eating, exercising, and resting are imperative. Spiritual growth includes prayer, Bible study, fellowship, witnessing, and worship.

Continue to look for team members committed to the vision.

Missionaries Mentoring

Each year, The Sowers Ministry trains thousands of leaders. They are added to the church and serve in their own nations. They are like native foot soldiers for Christ.

Some people have a vision for reaching the poor. Some will reach out to students, while others will have a heart for ministering to governmental officials. Others may have an interest in unbelievers in general.

Whatever the vision may be, your household should not be divided. Mark 3:25 states, "If a house is divided against itself, that house cannot stand." (7) In the Parable of the Sower, what inspired my ministry name, illustrated in Mark 4:16-17, Jesus said, "Others, like seed sown on rocky places, hear the word and at once receive it with joy. But since they have no root, they last only a short time. When trouble or persecution comes because of the word, they quickly fall away." Those who are insufficiently trained could be like those seeds that are planted in rocky soil. They may be excited about God's work, but they do not have a firm foundation or strong enough root system to survive the challenges that are certain to come. (7)

How did Jesus train people? He "called to him those he wanted…that they might be with him…that he might send them out…and to have authority to drive out demons…" (Mark 3:13-15). (7)

The Mentorship Style of Jesus:
1) Jesus Chose Them
2) Jesus Taught Them
3) Jesus Gave Them Experience
4) Jesus Empowered Them
5) Jesus Sent Them Out

Let's examine these points.

Choosing the Right People

Jesus did not necessarily choose those who were skilled. He chose those He wanted and those who were willing to follow Him. Mark 1:18 states, "At once they left their nets and followed him," and Mark 2:14 states, "...Follow me, Jesus told him, and Levi got up and followed him." These men were so eager to be with Him that they followed him "at once." (7)

Teaching

Jesus taught the disciples on a daily basis. They followed Him everywhere. They listened as He preached to the huge crowds. He spoke directly to them in greater depth when they were alone. He sometimes taught them in parables, and they were conditioned to be prepared for anything.

Numbers 27:18 reads, "So the Lord said to Moses, 'Take Joshua son of Nun, a man in whom is the spirit of leadership, and lay your hand on him.'" (7) Moses chose Joshua as a leader. He had the capabilities and spirit necessary for being a leader.

Moses discerned these qualities in Joshua and the Lord confirmed it.

Another "rule" for leaders is to choose those who go the extra mile. A person who has an attitude of service will respond to responsibility with eagerness, thanking the community for giving him the opportunity to serve them. That is leadership.

Enabling Trainees Experience

Jesus asked the disciples questions to make them think and to test and practice their faith. Examples include: Mark 8:29: "Who do you say I am?" and Mark 6:37-38: "You give them something to eat...how many loaves do you have?" (7)

By walking with Jesus, His disciples were able to experience His vision for the poor and lost. Consider the things they were exposed to: powerful healings (Mark 5:34, 5:41), driving out demons (Mark 5:8), signs and wonders (Mark 4:39), and miracles (Mark 6:30-44).

Empowering Others

Jesus gave power to His disciples. "Jesus called his twelve disciples to him and gave them authority to drive out impure spirits and to heal every disease and sickness." (Matt. 10:1)(7)

Matthew 10:1 and Acts 1:8 state: "But you will receive power when the Holy Spirit comes on you; and you will be my witness in Jerusalem and in all Judea, and Samaria and to the ends of the earth." (7)

What can leaders learn from this? Leaders should teach their disciples about this empowerment and pass it on through prayer and the laying on of hands as Scripture teaches us to do.

Sending Out Disciples

Jesus sent the disciples out. "These twelve, Jesus sent out with the following instructions," in Matthew 10:5 and "Therefore go and make disciples of all nations, baptizing them in the name of the Father and of the Son and of the Holy Spirit, and teaching them to obey everything I have commanded you. And surely I am with you always, to the very end of the age," in Matthew 28:19-20. (7)

Chapter 6: Leadership & Agents of God

When the disciples finished their training, Jesus sent them out with instructions. These instructions were basically this: to do for the world what He had done for them: make disciples, baptize, and teach everything Jesus had taught them. Therefore, Jesus was telling his disciples to train people as he had trained them. Likewise, we should follow Jesus' pattern of training also: choose, teach, allow experiences, empower, and send.

Additional Leadership Advice

1) Family Relationships

When a leader looks for a spouse, he or she should make sure their calling is clearly communicated and that the mate agrees with ministry principles. Leaders also need good relationships with their children. Many times this is reflected in the children wanting to follow in their parents footsteps. Balancing family and ministry is a skill. The true leader must genuinely care about people through sorrow, joy, and pain.

2) Goal Setting

Make your goals attainable regarding this subject. The late Pastor John Osteen used to say, "You must have ladders, but also remember that as a Christian you have the power of the Holy Spirit inside you. You do not have to look only to your human strength." (6) You must desire to achieve more for the Lord. "Goal-setting is an ongoing discipline of a true leader. Failure at this point destroys the confidence of followers because it destroys the credibility of the leader." (6) Dr. Paul Crites says, "Every leader knows that the secret of your future is hidden in your daily routine." (3)

3) Universal and Practical Habits

Understand what God is saying to you and believe Him.
Expect to make a big impact for Him.

Simplify your life to allow more time for God and more funds for mission work.

Have a desire to meet great people and know that some may be in your own neighborhood.

Regularly meet with and care for people in your life.

Go wherever a door of opportunity is opening up. For example, if a communist nation allows funding for natives to grow crops, be a support there and believe God for breakthrough for the gospel.

Know that desire must come from within. Wake up every day and ask God to show you what you can do for Him. I ask this question while being mindful that there are 3.5 billion people alive who have not heard the name of Jesus Christ. I also know that business people are one of the keys to confronting this challenge. I always desire to meet successful people. In most cultures, it is easy to meet ordinary people, but I expect to meet and have favor with people who are achieving success at the top of the corporate ladder. For example, meeting with leaders at Google or Yahoo that are interested in improving the conditions in North Korea or other parts of Asia.

Realize people cannot give if they do not have. Prosperity includes many aspects of life, but great wealth and money should also be expected from God and others. The Scripture states men shall pour wealth into our lives (Luke 6:38). I have found this is where many people fail.

Most people do not desire wealth for the right reasons related to the gospel. I want to encourage you to say, "God, I desire wealth." Expect other like-minded people to enter your life for fellowship and in order to invest in God's kingdom.

Some positive aspects about my upbringing are that I was not exposed to a lot of worldly influences and materialistic pressures. I learned about God and I obtained wealth at an early age. When I seriously committed my life to the Lord, I was in my twenties and God revealed to me that there was incredible wealth waiting for me to apprehend and invest into the kingdom of God. This empowering purpose fuels me to wake up early every morning. I want to challenge you to receive blessings in order to be a blessing in others' lives.

Sadly, I have seen the opposite side of people too. In fact, many large churches with very large budgets, give only 1 percent to missions. And only one cent out of every $100 is given to areas of the world where most people live and they happen to be unreached...*never having heard the gospel once!*

I thank God for the many faithful believers around the world who sacrificially give to TSM every year. The Scripture is true: the more we give, the more God gives back to us (Proverbs 11:24-25). This is encouraging in lieu of the fact that there are millions of people depending upon us to help them and to tell them the truth of the gospel.

It is my duty to expect God to work all things together for my good (Romans 8:28) and to bring the right business people across my path...*business people who are ready to listen to God, to give financially, and to make a difference in world missions.*

This attitude reflects hearts that are right. Knowing people who understand their value in Christ and their position in the kingdom is important. For the sake of the unreached poor people, desire the gift of faith (1 Corinthians 12:9), and know that God has called all of us to help in one manner or another. There are people waiting and wanting to help (Hebrews 11:6).

Maturing in Leadership

Leaders cannot be afraid of problems. Leaders must learn how to solve problems biblically. In order to develop in this area, we must read the Bible, pray, and write down thoughts that the Lord gives to help us.

We need to be kind during problem solving. We must address sin and other situations that can surface in the church. Jesus' principle and key was to love. Love resolves most problems. We should find opportunities to repent when we sin. God wants us to be pure before Him and serve Him with a clean heart.

Before entering into discussion with leaders, I pray. This is especially important when it involves dealing with an obstacle. That is maturity. Direct conversation with leaders is best, and I attempt to share my thoughts according to biblical views.

Good leadership comes with experience; therefore, I counsel people to take life step-by-step to deal with issues. Leaders are human too, so we must share God's love and allow repentance from the heart to the Lord. As leaders, we must be very careful with money, sexual sin, pride, and position. We must be mindful of equal rights as well.

The anointed leadership training that has been imparted into my life has brought me to the place where I can share my vision in a group or one by one. As the Bible instructs, we must write down the vision, pray over it, and share it. It is rewarding to find good leadership qualities in people and spend time equipping them. This equipping is a continual process. To see a vision come to pass, I must be willing to share it again and again. Sometimes it takes people a long time to grasp a vision.

Maturity is the most important success secret. Be a good example in life. Knowing the Bible is not good enough. There are many trials and temptations, but God will help if we pray and stay focused. As leaders, we must have godly people surrounding us to encourage us and pray for us. If we live differently than what we say or preach, it is of no use and brings shame to God's Name. Eventually, people will find God by observing our ways of living. It is wise to live in a godly way. We do not have to force something to happen in our own strength. God is in control and He will help us to be a qualified and mature leader.

Select people who desire to be good leaders. Find out about their character and ability to perform. They also must have a desire to excel, always be willing to learn, spend time in prayer, and develop confidence in their ability to share a vision from God. They must be people who trust God for the past, present, and future.

There is help from the Lord if someone is willing to pursue Him. Concerning leadership, a strong foundation in Him is the crucial key to build on.

Having fellowship with other leaders, sharing personal issues, and devotional time together is crucial. God is working in us to develop our character. There is always room to grow and learn from others. A leader that wants to get help and guidance from the Lord and develop a solid relationship with Him must pray two to three hours a day. Chinese leaders who are in the ministry pray three to four hours a day. My friend, Sister Chu, prays five to six hours a day! I learned to pray just by being with Chinese leaders.

Leaders fast and pray against generational curses. A strong prayer life is a key to being a good leader. God is watching to see how much we really want to be with Him and experience His presence. Often leaders do not spend enough time in prayer. So they are isolated and eventually become a victim of the enemy. They can lose everything...*even if they were a good, qualified leader.* I would highly recommend that leaders pray several hours or more per day to have a Spirit-filled and supernatural life in Christ Jesus.

We can especially influence people when we are able to help them in their times of need. People will feel God's love and follow Jesus when they are loved and cared for by His people.

A true leader wants to spend time with and mentor others. Influence then happens. When there is a crisis, a true leader sticks close by like a brother or family member. In China, a true leader wants to feed those he trains.

A potential leader is always watching other leaders and following the best example he or she can find. However, today many leaders are failing because they are not following Christ and have drifted away from the truth. Just as iron sharpens iron, God wants each leader to follow Him and to follow a good leader who has proven him/herself and led a life of sacrifice and quality. We must be a good example to others, so let us lead with honesty and the quality character of God.

To build healthy relationships, we need to spend time with others, care for them, demonstrate love, and go the extra mile for them. Relationships are always hard if we do not work hard at understanding each other. Love is a very important element of peaceful relationships. A good leader develops different levels of relationships, including those with a spouse, children, workers, a boss, or church members.

Managing money is a skill just like having relationships. A leader should know about and master this topic. Unfortunately, many leaders are not keen to learn or practice biblical ways of managing money. Learn from others and be a good example by living within your means. If God provides, then you can spend. *Discern* if you can afford something or if it is better to wait. Spending too much is not wise, because the Bible teaches us to be good and faithful stewards.

More from Neil

Westerners should come and visit China, North Korea, India, or Central Asia in order to see how believers live in such poor areas. Please come and bring good teaching to the church leaders. Also, help and pray for the younger generation to sincerely know and follow Jesus.

Western Christians, please take notice when persecution arises. Similarly, there is a huge need for help in caring for orphans and widows. How can they get help if Christians are not a good example or fail to reach out to them? A healthy church happens when a good leader finds God's Word to be true and is a doer of the Word. We must be obedient to His calling and pursue His rest in us.

Chapter 6: Leadership & Agents of God

China is the destination of most of my travels, but I have been led by the Holy Spirit to minister in different places, too. Chinese leaders are keen to learn from the West. I want to spend more time bringing the younger generation into leadership. It will take prayer, sacrifice, worship, fasting, and much more. Therefore, let us care for the committed leaders of our time.

As I discover and remember stories like the one that follows, I press on to see more of the greatness of God.

Missionary Lama of Tibet

When I first met Lama from Gangtok, (in Sikkim/Bhutan), he was a young man from a village. While he was very sick, the witch doctor had dedicated Lama to Satan and performed witchcraft on his family.

Lama escaped to India where he came across an evangelist who prayed for him. Lama immediately converted to Christianity. As it turns out, this evangelist was one of our leaders from our Mission Training Center (MTC).

Lama began waking up early in the morning to pray for his siblings whom he had not seen for years. He continued to live in a foreign land, but Lama knew God had a purpose for him.

One morning at the MTC, Lama had kitchen duty. It was the first time he had seen a gas stove. All his life, he had only seen people cook over a fire made of wooden sticks. At first, Lama thought he was seeing some kind of magic, so he had to be comforted.

Even though Lama had a very primitive background, an amazing event followed his conversion. In six months, Lama preached to literally hundreds of people. Four churches were started in order to teach all the people and to hold fellowships.

I wanted to share this to make the point that anyone who is teachable can have the potential to lead. Lama learned from the gospel that the Holy Spirit leads and helps in all situations. He decided to believe the Bible and act upon it. He wanted others to know about Jesus Christ, too.

Today, Lama is in charge of MTCs in India and Nepal.

Touching Muslims with God's Love: Pastor Chan

With tears in his eyes and strength in his voice, Pastor Chan boldly claims, "It is a privilege to suffer and to serve God." This faithful man of God is part of a powerful movement emerging within believers in the Chinese underground church.

Last month, we visited three of our centers in three provinces. We had the privilege to encourage the local believers and ministers at many house churches. We also held secret training seminars for the leaders who oversee the underground church movement.

These saints are praying and making inroads to bring the gospel back to Jerusalem.

Their goal is to reach the Tibetan and Muslim world for Christ. They believe that the severe persecution they have faced so far is preparing them for what they may face in the hands of Muslim extremists en route to Jerusalem. They are already reaching out to the radical Muslim community in Xinjiang Province. One province has over 200 Muslims converts who meet secretly to worship and learn more about Jesus.

One of these believers with a remarkable story is Pastor Chan.

Because of his open faith in Jesus, Pastor Chan was imprisoned in a Chinese labor camp for thirteen years. As a prisoner, he was sadistically tortured. To shame him, they paraded him through the city with a sign on his neck declaring that he was a follower of Christ. His earthly possessions were confiscated ten different times!

Despite intense persecution, Pastor Chan has steadfastly followed God. While imprisoned, his trust in the Lord enabled him to win half the prisoners to Christ!

Over the years, he started several house churches in rural areas of West China (Muslim populated areas). He still faces life threatening situations and imprisonment.

Six weeks ago, the authorities destroyed one of his churches, but he continues in his labor for the Lord. When asked what outside Christians can do to help, he simply said, "Please pray that we remain faithful to our Savior and reach the unreached."

Chapter 7: Women on a Mission

When I recently ministered in India, I witnessed many timid women who were too fearful to have hands laid on them or to pray for others. As I was writing this book, I felt the Lord nudge me to add another subject that is important for effective leadership in the Kingdom.

There are no differences between men and women in Christ (Galatians 3:28). We are all equal in the eyes of God. However, there are different roles within the Body of Christ (1 Corinthians 12:4-17).

Christ has given specific roles to each of us so that we may function properly within the Body of Christ (Ephesians 5:23).

Mary Magdalene delivered the good news to the disciples that Christ had risen (John 20:11-18).

The Holy Spirit used the prophet Anna to speak of the arrival of the Christ to all those who were looking for the redemption of Jerusalem (Luke 2:38).

Cast your religious teachings aside. The Holy Spirit used these women to bring new truths to all people...*including men.*

Women are a blessing to the Body of Christ. We should never tolerate an environment that produces an atmosphere where they are oppressed or fearful to minister to others. The role of women in ministry is also promoted in Titus 2:3-5, "Likewise, teach the older women to be reverent in the way they live, not to be slanderers or addicted to much wine, but to teach what is good. Then they can urge the younger women to love their husbands and children, to be self-controlled and pure, to be busy at home, to be kind, and to be subject to their husbands, so that no one will malign the word of God." (7)

Even considering the cultural traditions and times when this passage of Scripture was written, it has valuable truths for women today.

In Esther 4:9-17, a woman was faced with an opportunity to make a difference. Esther, a young Jewish woman who became the favorite of King Ahasuerus, was in a position to save her people from the evil that Haman had plotted against the Jews. It took a great deal of courageous leadership as well as extraordinary diplomacy for Esther to intervene. A single misstep in the male dominated Persian Empire could have cost Esther her life and the lives of thousands of her people.

We honor Esther because she took advantage of her relationship with the king in order to do good. Her relative, Mordecai, also escaped death, and the evildoer, Haman, died instead.

God's will came to pass because Mordecai and Esther believed in women serving God in leadership positions.

In Romans 16:1-16, the apostle Paul sends greetings to a list of men *and women*. Paul often encouraged women in the early church to be part of the team. He encouraged them to refuse limitations. In this chapter, he praises and commends women who worked by his side in the Lord. He expresses his gratitude for their gifts of encouragement, their personal support, and their leadership in the church.

We learn in Acts 18:2-3 that Priscilla and Aquila had left Rome when Emperor Claudius expelled the Jews. They traded a settled home life for the life of wanderers, supporting themselves in ministry as they moved from one city to another by their profession of tent making.

We also read about a woman named Phoebe at the beginning of Romans 16, whom Paul describes as "our sister, a deacon of the church at Cenchreae, and ... a benefactor of many people including me." (7)

All through the New Testament, we see women in leadership roles. Leadership is influence.

Most people want to make a difference...*including women*. Many are not sure how to go about doing it.

In some respects, women may have greater challenges to overcome than they have ever faced before. On the other hand, they have more opportunities to make an impact in communities, nations, and our world.

Women are usually the primary care providers for their families. Many powerful men of history attributed their value system to what they learned from their mothers and older sisters.

Effective leadership training is not only informational and inspirational but also, most important, it is transformational. It has been observed in the educational sector that people will forget what is being said or what their teacher does, but they remember how their leader made them feel.

Women are sometimes better at touching hearts. This can be beneficial in training others. I want to see more women teaching other young women about the principles of life. This is also important in third-world nations where the value of women and their leadership roles are usually held to be less than in civilized nations. As you continue to read this book, you will find testimonies and/or interviews from women in Christian leadership roles, who are continuing to make an impact in third-world nations around the earth.

Testimony by Amy Anderson

Like many ministers' families, our family sacrifices a lot of time, energy, and money for missions. When people submit to missionary work, a multitude of problems are solved. God is even able to supernaturally have financial debt canceled from accounts that are legitimate debt.

Mission work changed me. It made me really thankful for what I do have. It actually made me want to give away everything I had, as it brought a more correct perspective concerning material things. Mission work caused me grow into my ministry giftings of teaching and worship dance.

Basically, nothing can compare to mission work. It is called the Great Commission for a reason. There is protection and provision in doing God's will. Let me encourage you to go into every mission field with all your heart and simply tell your own testimony. Everyone has a testimony about God's goodness at one or more times in their lives. God miraculously healed me of chronic asthmatic bronchitis, gave me a unique gift of worship dance, and taught me how to stay well. Now, I want to tell the world that nothing is as great as our God!

While I am convicted and motivated to make a difference abroad, I am also concerned about my nation. I believe Americans need to give to the Great Commission like never before. It is probably our only real hope to secure our future as a free nation. Luke 6:38 clearly states that reaping and sowing is real. My husband, Neil, operates in a gift of faith, lives out of the fruit of peace, and listens and responds to wisdom from the Holy Spirit. He believes in the Scripture that states God's people have the power to get wealth (Deuteronomy 8:18).

My husband is very driven and disciplined. He wakes up early every morning thinking about how to care for the less fortunate Christians around the world. Something I have observed him doing is verbalizing specific, thankful prayers at least twice a day. He lives expecting good things to happen, seeks counsel from other Christian leaders who are achieving more than he is, and he reads the Psalms daily. These simple steps make a profound difference in his life and in those around him.

Let us believe together that we will choose to adopt some of the behaviors of successful Christians whose stories are throughout this book. Breakthroughs will happen for you, even in the midst of great trials, in order for you to give to the work of the Lord…*indefinitely.*

"Nations need you."

"Nations need Him."

I remember words from an article written by the late Kenneth E. Hagin, "It pays to obey, and it costs us if we do not." "Let us serve God with passion and hasten His return." (2 Peter 3:12) (7)

Sister G. Bi on China and Influence

In the year 2000, I became involved with The Sowers Ministry. Mature leadership was modeled in front of me that compelled me to lead in the same way.

Since then, I have learned a lot about Western mindsets concerning mission work. I personally think it is very important for a Chinese house church to have an adequate and appropriate leader. As I started to study the Bible, little by little I found reasons to be a good leader. The Chinese church is very important to me. I always wanted to learn to be a wise leader.

For a period of time, my older brother was my mentor, and I learned a lot from him due to his knowledge of the Bible. Sister Zhao in Shanghai is also my mentor, although, I do not meet with her face to face very often. Her teachings on the Word through an online blog have been most beneficial. She always answers my email if I have questions.

Neil Anderson is also a leader in my life and ministry. As I have worked with him and others, I have found that life is full of leadership training. He has taught me that I can always expect to be a better leader in future...*even if I am not perfect.*

Often I get opportunities to work with Western missionaries. Western mentalities are very different from the Chinese thought processes. I've learned that being a Christian is not superstition or brain washing. It is having a personal relationship with God. Being a Christian means striving to be the best in life.

Chinese house churches need good teachers and leaders. This is especially true for the younger generations. It is my desire to help the leaders in Chinese churches to mature in the things of God. This will cause rapid growth to occur.

Great leaders should be like Jesus: always gaining knowledge, eager to learn, maturing, and ready to serve people. They are also good communicators to both God and to His people. They are willing to teach others simple principles and live a lifestyle that reflects honesty and godly character. They do not live double lives.

It is my blessing to minister often in Chinese churches and mentor about 1,300 youth leaders. They love to serve the Lord and I help them learn how to follow the Lord and His commands. One of the most enjoyable things I do is working with Sister Chao who oversees more than 1,000 Christian leaders. There are other Christian leaders with whom I am in contact but cannot mention by name for safety's sake.

Advice of Pastor Sikala of India

The key Scripture that helped me to decide to become a minister of the gospel was Ephesians 4:11-13. God actually gave leadership gifts to certain people in order to prepare others to receive all that Christ died for us to have. I realized the Lord needs workers in the harvest field. In every neighborhood, town, city, state, and nation, the generals of the Lord's army need to lead. I help Christians attain leadership skills in churches in India where they are desperately needed.

A godly leader/mentor will provide the necessary guidance to help people avoid certain pitfalls. Ministry leaders soon learn how to overcome the challenges that spring forth. My parents were my first mentors. I am grateful to my father for his ministry, as he taught me certain values that were essential for a successful life of honesty, integrity, and hard work.

A great leader is compassionate and equipped with the spiritual and natural abilities to overcome all obstacles. God uses ordinary people to do extraordinary work. We can all be great leaders in life. We must work diligently with honesty, ethics, and integrity, and make an honest effort to think about the needs of others. We must pray consistently and learn from the Holy Spirit. We should teach on the gifts of God and always have our minds set on God. We must go the extra mile to love and care for others who are in the family of God.

Our leadership team has learned a few lessons after one year of prayer, preparation, and leadership training. We felt led to start a women's ministry, and now we have a successful women's mentoring team at our church. Our biggest priority is learning to trust God. Establishing and sustaining any ministry is a consistent exercise in faith and reliance upon the Lord.

Leadership is a learning process, too. We give ourselves room to fail and grace to try again. We encourage each other on the journey. We fast during the week and ask the Lord to help us. Many people are being persecuted, tortured, and looked down upon because of their faith in Christ. The untouchable, lower-class believers are especially vulnerable to this problem.

There is no limit to how many people I can mentor as long as I serve the Lord and remain in good relationship with His people. My constant goal is to guide them in godly ways. Each year I mentor over one hundred leaders. Pastors and leaders are dear to my heart. They can serve better if we can love and help them in their trials and hardship. Doing this is one of the reasons why the church is growing in India. We have seen a thirty percent increase in people being baptized each month. The spirit of revival has been here for the last ten years. Many evangelists are going out and saving lost souls.

Patience is the key for solving problems. Having right leadership skills to analyze the cause of problems is also important. Observation for any possible clues to solve a problem is a must when you don't know how to fix a situation. We pray as a team and share thoughts, because big problems need much prayer and guidance from the Lord.

Chao of Shanghai: Miracle, Prison, & Family Restored

Sister Chao was born and brought up in a very low class family. Her father had been killed in The Cold War when she was only 16 years old. From that day on, her life was spent begging on the streets for the survival of her family. Her life seemed like she was living in hell.

In 1982, she gave her life to God and dedicated herself to the work of missions.

Sister Chao dreamed about having a godly husband, but she was afraid to pray for the best. However, God revealed to her that He would be faithful to her because of her commitment to Him. With the Lord's help, she met a wonderful and kind husband who worked for the government. In spite of her desperate situation, she married and soon had a baby boy.

Unfortunately, her son was diagnosed with a rare blood disease and had no mobility whatsoever. He also suffered with constant pain, and Chao felt helpless. One day, her son appeared to be dying. So she and her husband rushed their baby boy to the nearest hospital so he could be treated. They had to take a train, and hours later, they arrived and saw a doctor.

They doctor immediately ordered a blood transfusion, but the hospital was unable to match his blood type. In this high-risk situation, the only option was to pray and trust the Lord. The Lord heard the prayers of the righteous. Chao and her husband were relieved when their son did not die, but they were also very saddened because he was crippled.

All the joy was gone from Chao's family. The little boy began to grow abnormally, and his care took up most of their time and attention.

Everyday life became very stressful, and soon Chao and her husband began to quarrel daily. Finally, they decided to get a divorce. Chao took her son and moved far away from her husband. A few years later, on China's National holiday, Chao's friends took her to a house church meeting. When she entered the church, she saw a cross and immediately her heart became full of joy. Then Chao began weeping as she recalled how she used to love the Lord. The problems of the world had taken over her life and her heart was full of sorrows and had become cold.

The believers there then surrounded her and started to pray for her and her son. He was growing up, but was still unable to walk or talk. Her son was six-years-old and he often looked for his father.

Chao began to pray and asked the Lord to forgive her and renew her relationship once again with Him.

When Chao got back home that day, her son suddenly jumped out of her lap and started to walk. It was a tremendous miracle after so many years of suffering.

She thanked the Lord the whole night.

The next day she contacted her husband and told him what had happened. She then asked for forgiveness from him as well. Her husband accepted her back. They reunited and began to serve the Lord together.

Chao eventually completed Bible training and started working with a famous house church leader, Pastor Wang Ming Dao. He had spent nearly twenty-three years in prison for his faith. Chao then spearheaded the printing of three million copies of a Christmas tract with a gospel message and distributed it free of cost throughout twenty-nine of the provinces in China.

After the gospel literature distribution, Chao was arrested by the security police and sentenced to three-and-one half years in prison. While there, she was forced to work eighteen-hour days. The room she lived in was only fourteen square meters (about 150 square feet) and shared with fourteen other prisoners! There was a toilet in the room, but no one had privacy. Food was scarce; they were only given rice and one vegetable daily. She also had to wake up at for work at 5 a.m.

During the time she was imprisoned, twenty-eight people prayed to receive Jesus Christ as their Lord and Savior. She baptized four people, and wrote 5,040 letters to her parents and friends about the Word of God. Whenever the police became aware of this, she was beaten and removed to an even more secluded area of the prison called the Secret Cell.

Finally, on December 28, she was freed from prison. Today Chao is busy leading a house church along with her husband. They help many leaders by going out and evangelizing.

Chao says, "I have gone through much pain in my life, but now I know true peace and joy as I live for the Lord. Pray for my family, church, and ministry in China."

Bible Women of Jilin, North China

A few years ago in Jilin, China, a pastor of a church suddenly died and left the congregation to fend for themselves, spiritually and physically. Several women came together and made a promise to seek the Lord daily and to witness to the lost souls in the surrounding countryside. Before they began, they fasted for an entire week and heard the Lord tell them that He was going to ensure that the Good News would be proclaimed. Having heard from God, they felt confident and reassured that they had nothing to fear.

Today, these women are as strong and diligent as ever. They are fervent about their calling, and every single day, without any interference or excuse, they take the gospel to the people.

Together, they are known as "The Bible Women" because they not only share God's Word with the unsaved, they have endured many ordeals to distribute and provide Bibles to both new believers and leaders.

Two of "The Bible Women" have gone through tremendous grief when their husbands were imprisoned for their faith. Nevertheless, they refrain from talking about it and concentrate on sharing the love of God with those who have never heard the Name of Jesus.

Please keep these strong women of faith in your prayers as they have dedicated their lives to the calling the Lord has given them. They travel great distances in order to pick up Bibles for new converts. Often times they will wait for as long as two whole days for Bibles to arrive at the delivery station platform.

Thank you for praying for angels of protection to gather about and for partners to come alongside and support them as they provide these precious Bibles.

The province where these ladies minister is experiencing revival. More than 20 percent of the population there is Christian.

In order to disciple the growing number of new believers, The Bible Women are in dire need of more Bibles in Jilin.

Thirty-eight Churches Planted and Counting: Shung H.S.

Shung H.S. lives in Harbin, China, with her husband and their two children. She accepted Jesus Christ as her Lord and Savior at thirty years of age and has served in ministry for seven years. From the moment she first read the Bible, Shung has had a passion to reach others and share the love of Jesus Christ with everyone she knows and meets. She often thinks of all the years of her life that she wasted and has a desire to make up for all the time that she has lost.

Shung has been able to plant 38 churches where she visits and preaches the Word of God. She holds Bible studies and fellowship services that usually last six to seven hours. New believers are hungry to learn from her. The churches are new and always full of activities.

Shung has a special passion for the university students in her area. She says that many of them are searching for truth and knows that the only source for unadulterated truth is the Bible. She states, "How will they know unless someone is sent and tells them? How will they know Jesus unless someone expresses the true love of God to them?"

Shung is committed to learning more from and about the Word of God herself so that she can faithfully teach new believers. She is a diligent soldier in the army of God. Her personal conviction is to preach the Word in its entirety. She needs to stay strong due to the many false prophets that come to China. They come spreading a false gospel to the people. Sister Shung is determined and passionate about preventing new believers from being deceived; she believes in teaching and imparting a strong foundation.

Shung's initial Christian education was provided by The Sowers Ministry. Her training lasted six months and equipped her to be an effective leader. She said, "It was one of the best things I was able to do."

She explained that her time with The Sowers Ministry enabled her to fully comprehend God's Word, to mature in Christ, and to be strengthened in her faith. The training challenged her to fulfill her calling to plant and mobilize churches.

She also met many new friends in Christ. "It was a life-changing experience that I would definitely recommend," she concluded.

Now Shung and her teams train 1,200 young leaders at a time.

Shung and her associates covet your prayers and support in order to establish seven training centers in other provinces.

May the Lord help Pastor Shung continue to build His kingdom.

Chapter 8: Discipline, Money and Stewardship

Neil's Testimony Continued...

A little while ago, my wife, Amy, and I visited my father in India. He showed us the well where he used to draw water to carry in order to give my brothers and I a bath. After the death of my twenty-five-year-old mother, my dad had to care for four sons who were all under six years of age.

This life eventually became too difficult for him. Now, I realize why. On top of everything else, he had no electricity or running water.

However, today he loves to recall how God helped him in those days. He is happy to reflect.

When I was four, my father enlisted the help of a Methodist orphanage, run by dedicated Christian women, to care for us. Looking back, I am so thankful for my father's humility and for the Methodist women who loved me into the Christian faith.

From the sisters, B.P. and C.P., at the orphanage, I learned about working hard and eventually graduated from a university. My vision was to be in business. Looking into my future, I saw the world was a place for me to succeed, and I set a goal of becoming a medical doctor.

At age seventeen, I started my career and prospered in every business I worked in, even the Bollywood film industry!

Growing up as a youth in India, I witnessed many individuals addicted to drugs. Sometimes I even experimented with them. Coming from a mixed background, the worldly gained wealth soon fed my need for more drugs. As a young adult, I was spiritually lost and searching for peace. I planned a visit to Nepal for a drug connection and to visit my brother, whom I had heard was a new believer and was doing mission work.

Upon arrival in Nepal, I ended up in a small church, where the pastor was preaching on the Scripture, "Seek first the kingdom of God and His righteousness and everything will be added to you," (Matthew 6:33). That same day, I accepted Jesus as my personal Savior. I responded to the call of mission work made clear in Scripture, "Go into all the world and preach the gospel." (7)

At that moment, I was compelled to leave everything I had earned behind. To this day, I have no idea what became of the significant ill-gotten gains. I never returned to find out.

My brothers also experienced salvation, and in 1986, we planted Victory churches in Asia along with The Sowers Ministry. Ours was a very small beginning. We all had passion and the inextinguishable fire of God within us. Often we had no food and only a very primitive shelter. I learned then that if the world was to hear the gospel, I must ask the Lord to bless us with wisdom and finances.

One of the main reasons leaders fail is because they do not understand the value of time or money. As leaders, we need to learn and develop the skills to be a blessing to the world. God has proven Himself to be very faithful to me. I am in my third decade of learning from Him and helping the poor with finances.

Good stewardship is also a key to growth in Kingdom business. It is not that difficult to learn. As leaders, we should truly want to reach the world. To do this we must be good stewards of the money entrusted to us.

Downsizing material possessions is helpful many times and a time saver.

I recommend leaders make a list of how they want to simplify their lives (e.g., watching less television or only shopping for necessities). Then, as they are able to give more financial support to missions, they should expect a 30, 60 and 100-fold return from and for the Kingdom of God.

The more we receive, the more responsibility we have. Balance is so important when it comes to material needs.

Stewardship is a vital part of Christianity. This chapter is for leaders who want to teach on this subject. Missionary David Livingstone, who died in Zambia, said, "I place no value on anything I have or possess except in relation to the Kingdom of God."

So what is stewardship? It is the management of resources on behalf of the owner. Let's read King David's prayer in 1 Chronicles 29: 14-18. "But who am I, and who are my people, that we should be able to give as generously as this? Everything comes from you, and we have given you only what comes from your hand. We are foreigners and strangers in your sight, as were all our ancestors. Our days on earth are like a shadow, without hope. LORD our God, all this abundance that we have provided for building you a temple for your Holy Name comes from your hand, and all of it belongs to you. I know, my God, that you test the heart and are pleased with integrity. All these things I have given willingly and with honest intent. And now I have seen with joy how willingly your people who are here have given to you. LORD, the God of our fathers Abraham, Isaac and Israel, keep these desires and thoughts in the hearts of your people forever, and keep their hearts loyal to you. God owns everything that we own. We even belong to Him. Everything we have and steward are His." (7)

It is important to acknowledge and to dedicate all our possessions to God, who is the real owner.

What are we stewards of? Every blessing we have has been given to us by God, so we are stewards. "Every good and perfect gift is from above, coming down from the Father..." James 1:17). (7) Therefore, every dollar, skill, minute, or good situation is given to us by God, and we must steward them wisely and faithfully.

The Bible says everyone will give an account to God of what we have done with what He has entrusted to us. Hopefully, He will say, "Well done, good and faithful servant. You have been faithful with a few things. I will put you in charge of many things. Come and share in your master's happiness!" (Matthew 25:21) (7)

"Whoever can be trusted with very little can also be trusted with much." (Luke 16:10) (7) Many people are not faithful in small things. There are those who want to start from the top and be in the leading position immediately. Some do not want to waste time discipling one person because they think they should be leading hundreds.

God wants us to first be faithful in smaller things and then He will reward us with more. We also need to focus on small beginnings. The Bible says we should not despise small beginnings. Jesus was born in a manger!

Accept what God has given you and do not compare yourself with others. In the parable of the talents, the man with less did not take from the man who had more. Instead, he used what he had. He did not complain to his master about his small amount. A leader should be satisfied with what he has from the Lord.

It is not what you have been given, but what you do with what you have. The servant in the book of Matthew was not judged by how much he began with, or how much he finished with, but by whether or not he was faithful with the things he was given. In Matthew 25, the master used the same praise words for both men despite how much they were given initially. He did not judge them by how much each man earned.

Instead, he saw each man was equally faithful with what he had been given. God looks at what you have been given and what you do with it. The person who is given more should do more. The man that is given less will probably have less required of him. God does not appreciate a miracle healer of thousands more than a teacher of three people if both are faithful with what they have been given.

Today, many Christians are called to distant lands, but many also walk away from the calling, the truth, and the priorities in this kingdom. This reminds me of a familiar Scripture, "When the young man heard this, he went away sad, because he had great wealth." (Matthew 19:22) Many western nations have not really given generously to mission work. The Bible also states, "Where your treasure is, there your heart will be also." (Matthew 6:21)(7) That is what I was taught as a new believer in church.

Financial Stewardship

Financial stewardship is looking after and managing money, and the things that money buys, which someone else has given over into your charge. Money is a substance that requires good stewardship. When God is the manager of our lives, He gives us the ability to care for those things entrusted to us. A godly leader is a good financial steward.

The following are critical for financial success:
- Set financial goals.
- Pay your tithe and offering first, then bills, and then save if you can.
- Be patient. Ask God to bless your seed as you give to God first.
- Spend less so you can give more to church and missions work.
- Prepare a budget.
- Avoid borrowing.*
- Use a credit card when needed in emergencies.
- Take responsibility for earning and proper spending.
- Be wise (Luke 16:11 & Matt 25:21).
- Live a simple life without excess materialism.
- Pay your taxes to honor those in authority over you.

The following are consequences of NOT giving:
- Robs God and does not access His promises (Mal. 3: 8)
- Brings a curse (Mal. 3: 9-12; Prov. 28: 27)
- Invites devourers (Mal. 3: 11)
- Stunts spiritual growth and increases negative challenges as Christians and leaders find their relationship with God affected
- Limits vision
- Causes a lack of accountability
- Brings more debt

* One way to be a good financial steward is to avoid debt. Aim to live within your means and plan to achieve financial freedom! If you are in debt, plan to get out of debt soon! Aim for financial freedom. A borrower is technically a slave to the lender (see Proverbs 22:7; 1 Corinthians 7:23). God's people should not be slaves to others. They should be financially free (Proverbs 11:24). Consider a Christian financial advisor.

Blessings from God

The Bible tells us that Christ died so that we could have life and abundance. (John 10:10) God never forces His blessings on people. Instead, He tells us how we can choose to receive them. This is also part of good stewardship. Let's choose God's blessings.

In the Old Testament book of Deuteronomy, we read about the blessings and curses that God allowed the children of Israel to experience. Chapter 28 lists all the blessings that would come on them for obeying God and all the curses that would happen if they did not. In Chapter 30, we read that if the curses came on them, they should repent and remember the blessings. Then, God would again bring His blessings upon them.

Chapter 8: Discipline, Money and Stewardship

Before we can enjoy God's blessings, we have to choose them. Deuteronomy 30:15 says, "See, I set before you today life and prosperity, death and destruction." (7) The choice is ours, and by making the decision to obey Him and receive His blessings we make the first step toward a good life and godly stewardship.

When we choose to enjoy God's blessings, we are also choosing to accept the problems and responsibilities that come with them. Jesus said, "...everyone who has been given much, much will be demanded; and from the one who has been entrusted with much, much more will be asked." (Luke 12:48)(7)

The second step to enjoying God's blessings is that we must be willing to accept the responsibility that comes with them.

Are you trustworthy? As a leader, an important step to take in preparation for greater blessings is to be faithful, or trustworthy, with what you currently have. How faithful are you when it comes to giving your time, talents, and treasures to God? Jesus said, "Whoever can be trusted with very little can also be trusted with much, and whoever is dishonest with very little will also be dishonest with much." (Luke 16:10) (7)

God wants to be sure that His blessings will be properly handled. When God plants a seed, He expects it to grow and multiply. It's the same with His blessings. He gives them to us so that we can share and multiply them. The next step to enjoying God's blessings is to be trustworthy with what we have and share our blessings with others so that they may increase. Luke 6:38 says to give and it shall be given back to you. This is another law of stewardship. Concerning the kingdom of God, some even say, "You can only keep what you give away."

Do you remember God when you should? In the parable of the sower, Jesus talked about how some of the seed was sown in the midst of thorns. The thorns choked out the seedlings and they did not bear much fruit. One of the "thorns" that He talked about was the "deceitfulness of wealth." (Mark 4:19) (7) If we are to enjoy much fruit and God's blessings, then we need to be careful to avoid being deceived by riches.

Deuteronomy 8:10-11 says, "When you have eaten and are satisfied, praise the LORD your God for the good land he has given you. Be careful that you do not forget the Lord your God, failing to observe his commands, his laws and his decrees that I am giving you this day."(7)

Riches deceive us whenever we fail to remember that it is God who gave us the ability to get them, even if it is just the riches we enjoy from our current job. Whenever we believe that we did it on our own, we choke out the fruit and cannot enjoy His blessings. One of the most important steps for us to make is to remember that all we have and all that we will receive comes from God...*and we are to always praise and thank Him for it..*

Authentic Christian leaders live and trust in God every day. We walk with Him daily. What a privilege it is.

Stewardship requires knowledge of, obedience to, and faith and trust in God. I believe giving toward the Great Commission accomplishes the highest level of godly stewardship. Giving while you are living is a sure way to live a purposeful life. First Timothy 6:17 states, "Command those who are rich in this present world not to be arrogant nor to put their hope in wealth, which is so uncertain, but to put their hope in God, who richly provides us with everything for our enjoyment." (7)

Legacy of Dr. P.P. Job by Neil Anderson

I became a serious disciple of Jesus Christ while in Nepal. In 1983, while attending a Christian meeting, a *Tortured for Christ* newsletter landed in my hands. Back then, it was illegal to have Christian work in Nepal or Tibet. After reading the newsletter, the Spirit of God touched my heart. I was compelled to write to the author, Dr. P.P. Job, in Green

Park, New Delhi. By reading a simple newsletter, God birthed a tremendous motivation in my heart to help persecuted Christians.

When Dr. Job learned that my brothers and I were all missionaries with a burden for China, he came and visited us in Kathmandu, Nepal. At that time, China's relationships with other countries, like Tibet, were very sensitive. After much prayer, in 1984, the doors for the gospel to be preached in these areas began to open slowly.

Dr. Job continued to come once a month and encourage us for several years. He also helped me bring the gospel to Tibet. He printed Tibetan Bibles and Christian literature by Richard Wurmbrand for distribution.

The Spirit of God and Dr. Job had prepared me for the trails that I would later face. Dr. Job had shared with me how he had traveled in China and worked among the persecuted believers. The experiences and stories he shared taught me so much! His humble spirit helped me become a leader. A spirit-led leader will teach others who are ready for ministry.

Later, I traveled to China with Dr. Job where he preached to thousands of leaders in Shanghai and in other rural areas. His heart was for the persecuted saints. There he met Sister Chu and preached in her church.

He also met and prayed for a widow who had been imprisoned for twenty-five years for her faith in Christ. After being severely tortured and humiliated, she was released and helped plant many churches!

Later, Delhi, India became our home and office headquarters. We officially launched the ministry there. Thousands of young leaders were trained, a monthly magazine called Lighthouse was mailed out, books were published, and CDs were distributed.

On several occasions, I had the opportunity to travel with Dr. Job to Europe and China. These were invaluable experiences for me because he was such a humble man of God. In my time spent with him, I learned that a harvest of souls does not come without paying a price and making great sacrifices in life.

Three years ago, Dr. Job came to my home in Houston, Texas, and encouraged me to take the gospel to North Korea. Like Rev. Wurmbrand, his heart was for the severely persecuted. The Bible states, "How can we forget such a great love?" I am a witness that Dr. Job truly understood the love of Jesus extending out to hostile nations.

Dr. Job has gone on to heaven. I truly miss him, as he was an inspiration to me and many others. He never gave up despite the incredible hardships he faced. The message of hope that he carried was personal, powerful and nation changing. Will there be anyone to carry on the vision Dr. Job had? Will there be anyone to follow in his footsteps, since his sons, Michael and John, were called home early?

I am sure Dr. Job's reward in heaven is great and he is finally reunited with his sons who died in tragic ways. May the Lord find us to be faithful like Dr. P.P. Job. He was always busy doing his Master's work!

Good and Faithful Servant: Jiang R.

In Huangpu, China, the Christian church is growing with many faithful believers. However, they face many needs. Many do not have access to a Bible and each day persecution occurs at some level.

During times of severe persecution, death is not uncommon. Yet, God's faithfulness is helping diligent leaders to serve believers there so the underground church is able to thrive.

Among the leaders is Pastor Jiang R. He grew up in a Christian home and this enabled him to have a solid foundation that would later help him in his ministry. After receiving Jesus Christ as his Lord and Savior, Pastor Jiang gave his life to the service of God's people. He started by studying under the leadership and guidance of his parent's ministry.

Chapter 8: Discipline, Money and Stewardship

Under his mom and dad's influence, he learned to serve and lead with diligence. Eventually, he started leading his own house church.

Surprisingly, he realized that he did not know enough of the Word of God and became motivated to study the Scriptures. He also wanted to visit some Christian training centers in order to grow in knowledge of the Word of God and be better able to encourage other believers.

As he did this, Pastor Jiang's knowledge of God grew he began to see the vital role churches play in the growth of the kingdom. The church was God's original plan. Pastor Jiang now understood that the Lord intended to build His church on the foundation of Jesus Christ. As he grew in the Lord and served his people, God blessed him and showed him favor.

Because of the extreme favor of God on his life, he was soon facing opposition from some government officials. At this point, the police started putting pressure on him. He also began to face personal trials. His health suddenly declined and he did not have enough money to pay for medical treatments.

When he applied for government assistance, he received the equivalent of only $20 USD a month! But Pastor Jiang kept his faith in the Lord. He prayed steadfastly to God and trusted that all his needs would be met. The Lord heard his prayers and proved His faithfulness once again by showing him favor. As he led and served God's people, doors of opportunity opened and God continued to provide.

Pastor Jiang faithfully continued the work that the Lord had given him to do. He began to travel to nine neighboring provinces. As he traveled, he saw an overwhelming lack among the people and a need for Bibles.

Burdened, he approached other leaders in hopes that they could help him, but they themselves were in rural parts of the country and struggling. *Even the government churches could not help*

Still, he knew the Lord would help him and make a way. As he trusted in the Lord, he was able to buy Bibles from an organization. However, this presented a new challenge. He bought so many Bibles that they had to be packed into heavy loads. One time, he made a trip that involved transporting thirty-five boxes filled with Bibles. Pastor Jiang did have help, but they had to carry each box up six flights of stairs to the location of a secret church meeting.

There were others trials too. The more they brought Bibles into the building, the more people noticed him. Eventually, a resident in the building reported his unusual behavior to the authorities.

Pastor Jiang was caught, heavily fined, and sent to prison for two years.

The prison conditions were harsh. In Northern China's winter months, some prisoners died of hypothermia from the below-freezing temperatures. In addition to his horrible environment, Pastor Jiang faced more persecution in prison! He was routinely threatened with death because of his Christian faith.

Despite opposition, he trusted in the Lord, knowing that somehow God would take care of him. Jiang made a vow to God that he would evangelize wherever he was, so he always brainstormed and searched for ways to talk to people about Jesus—even in prison. He was encouraged when he found a group of fellow believers in prison and began praying with them regularly. The meetings put the believers at increased risk for further persecution or death, but God protected the group.

Ultimately, they had favor as they shared the gospel with their fellow inmates. Their diligence and obedience to God's Word allowed them to witness to many people, and in one year, 1,213 souls came into the kingdom of God.

Pastor Jiang has been serving in his local churches for decades. The home churches serve as bases where over 150,000 believers meet regularly. He and his team also travel into several provinces to encourage other believers. They research and help find provisions for those in need. Each year they supply thousands of Bibles and teaching materials to Christian leaders in the villages they visit.

Pastor Jiang stated he is so thankful to foreign friends who make sacrifices and are willing to face dangerous situations to bring these valuable resources to them.

Today Pastor Jiang serves and shares the gospel throughout Northern China. He is blessed, anointed, and highly favored. His team thrives under his leadership. There is still much work to be done. Pastor Jiang's vision and goal is to reach those who have not yet heard the Good News. The team knows that as more believers come into the kingdom, more Bibles are needed for them to grow in their faith.

They continue to pray in faith and work to provide Bibles so believers can mature spiritually. He and his team encourage other believers to fast and pray for ways that they can provide Bibles.

Following the apostles in the book of Acts, the believers not only pray in faith, they give in faith. "It's a family affair," Pastor Jiang says of the collective commitment the believers have toward one another. Many sell large portions of their crops or livestock to help provide Bibles and training for new leaders.

"We want to build strong churches in China and everyone can play a part. We know that only the Word of God will change lives," comments Pastor Jiang.

Despite Tragic Losses, the Wangs Kept Their Faith

The Wangs have lived and ministered in the Jilin Province of Northern China for many years. Despite many hardships, God has continued to prove Himself faithful and sovereign to them through it all.

Before they were Christians, they had a son who died at a very young age. In the midst of this heartache, God revealed Himself to them. During those difficult days, they heard, received, and were comforted with the gospel message. They accepted Jesus Christ as their Lord and Savior and committed their lives to serving Him. Three years later, while serving in love and obedience to God, they had another son.

The Wangs continually share their testimony of faith and hope with everyone around them. They have followed God's leading into the ministry including evangelizing and doing other gospel work. Now, God has blessed their ministry and they continue to see God work in mighty ways.

Brother Wang has also trusted God with his professional goals as well. He started his own business and it has prospered. Clearly, he has the favor of God upon him and his business. He has been very successful and has even invited a friend to partner with him in his business.

However, another challenge was in Wang's future. Wang and his partner worked well together and their business thrived for years. But somehow, greed started to grow in the heart of Wang's friend who demanded a larger share in the company.

When Brother Wang declined the request, his friend and business partner gave in to temptation and ran off with the equivalent of $27,000 USD. To this day, Wang has never heard from his friend and the money has not been returned.

Wang and his wife continue to pray in faith that God will take care and provide for them. They know that with Him, nothing is impossible. Even though a financial hardship occurred, they continue to earnestly believe and pray for a miracle. They believe that one day the money that was stolen from them will be returned.

Currently, Wang is working in full-time ministry. He commits his resources to the work of God, including caring for the needy. Brother Wang and his wife travel throughout more than thirteen provinces. They preach and teach the Word of God. Even though they have encountered great difficulties, losing their son, and a significant amount of money, they continue to look to God for guidance.

Brother and Sister Wang's lives reflect Christ and shine like bright lights in dark places as they share the gospel and serve believers in China. Their hearts' desire is to distribute Bibles to new believers in order to increase truth and spiritual growth within their nation.

Farmer's Family Delivered by the Hand of God in Vietnam

A farmer who grew vegetables and worked a fish pond dreamed of starting a small business.

So he went to a loan shark to get the money needed to start his small business. Every morning he went to the market to sell vegetables and fish. Over the next few months, business was going okay, but he was not making enough money. The debt owed to the loan shark continued to increase. The loan shark told him that he would have three months to pay back what he owed or everything of value that he owned would be taken away.

Three months passed and the loan shark saw there was nothing of value to take. He persuaded the parents to give up their fourteen-year-old daughter so that she could go to work at a factory in the city. Reluctantly, the parents agreed.

Tragically, instead of working at a factory, the daughter was sold into prostitution. When the mother heard what had happened to her daughter, she was devastated. She thought, "How could I be such a bad mother?" The heartbroken mother became suicidal.

She tried to commit suicide but was rescued by some Christian believers who brought her to the saving knowledge of Jesus. Over time, the father also was saved.

With help, the family was able to pay a ransom and buy back their daughter's freedom. Through this, the whole family in the village was saved.

Now, the daughter is doing well with her studies at the university. She plans to use her knowledge to help grow vegetables and work the fish pond so her family can sustain themselves. The father remains amazed at how God turned something so evil into something good!

Chapter 9: Men Behind the Vision: Adopting Behaviors & Expecting Impartation

This chapter highlights certain behaviors and people who have invested in The Sowers Ministry over the years. They also expect impartation. Their partnership with us has been invaluable. They have not only sown financially, but have also given of their time and prayers. It is a privilege to serve God alongside them. Together we are doing great things for the kingdom of God.

To be successful, you need friends that God divinely connects to you. "Before you know it, your list [of friends] will grow just by" referrals from existing friends. Trust the Lord will attract the right business people to your cause and befriend them. Wait until they ask you about your cause before volunteering information to them. Seek God ahead of time for introduction lines to say. Ten hours per week is essential to make new contacts. Refer interested people to your website where you publish useful information regularly. Consider mailing updates or newsletters out consistently to key supporters and give public talks as God leads you to. If you stop receiving support from a giver for three months or more, delete them from your mailing list until they cross your path again.

Increasing someone's value means give first rather than "ask for" first. It means helping others so that they will look forward to helping you back. Define to yourself exactly what you are seeking or it will not get clearly communicated to the person you are connecting with. Remember, "good things come to those who have patience, and take consistent, persistent actions toward what they want. Make a list of the people you want to meet that will help you get what" God has put on your heart and "who you already know that might help you" connect to them. Then develop your contacts into relationships.

"To achieve your goals…be a person of action. People reluctant to connect are [either]…unprepared,…fearful of rejection,…[or]lack positive self-image/esteem. Courage is a self-inflicted quality that gains momentum every time you try it. Tell stories. Stories help people relate…" and in turn, they will most likely tell you a story too. With all these behavior changes, expect God to supernaturally intervene and daily verbalize thankfulness to Him for the outcomes you need. Surround yourself with a circle of Godly mentors that you can phone or visit that will pray and encourage you with the edifying words when you have down days. (15)

Wade's Concrete Business, Texas

While I have been in the concrete business for more than ten years, I must inform you I have had no business training at all. Actually, I went to school to be a pilot.

At one point in my life, I went on a mission trip to Mexico. It took only one day there for me to learn that I was not called to be a missionary. Later, I contemplated pastoring, but I did not have the skills to lead people. So, because of these experiences, I learned early in life the difference between those who are sent and those who send.

Through experience, I learned we all reap what we sow. No matter what a person believes, we all get the opportunity to make a difference in life.

However, there is an anointing to make money and to fund the kingdom of God. Without money, we are crippled and cannot get things done. Because of this anointing for finances, I can be comfortable with making money and funding organizations like The Sowers Ministry. My business does well when I am obedient in my giving to God.

Chapter 9: Men Behind the Vision: Adopting Behaviors & Expecting Impartation

One year, everything shut down. For three months I had no work. I literally had only $30 USD in my business account and $0 in my other accounts. There was nothing left to do but listen to the Lord.

God spoke to me over a three-day period. Diligently, I wrote out what the Holy Spirit was speaking to my inner man: "If you will do things my way and quit doing things the way you think they should be done, one year from now you will not even recognize your business. It will be different and successful." As I attempted to obey and continually sought God's counsel, changes started happening for the better.

People began to tell me tell me that I had a gift to do things well. Really, what I do is take what *God* is doing and make money from that to help others fulfill their vision. During one season, another stream of income occurred. God gave me another business by giving me an idea. Under His direction, I started installing fireplaces.

Shortly after, increased favor manifested when a man came to me and said he had too much business. He gave me his customers! My steps must have been ordered, because I was in the right place at the right time and ran into the right man. This could not have occurred in the natural realm. Later, we bought his business for a fraction of the cost of what it was worth. There is no doubt in my mind that God wants His children to succeed.

God told me once, 'I don't need another rich man. I want someone able to handle money and fund missions. What good is money if people don't know how to use it for the kingdom?' God is looking for someone who is in relationship with Him and walk in obedience. I do not just want people that walk in prosperity, but in power with signs and wonders following. It is an anointing and a calling, not just an opportunity.

The new generation, the next great awakening, can happen in the marketplace. Walk in the light and see miracles happen. Prosperity will find you like a magnet. The stronger the power, the stronger the pull.

We cannot build the kingdom with our carnal minds. We will build it with our spirits as righteous men. Pray, follow, and overtake. Do not allow the world to overtake you with carnal thinking.

R. W., President of H. A., Houston, Texas

As a businessman and a believer, I consider mission work as a keystone of my giving. For most people, as third and fourth generation citizens of America, it can be difficult to travel to third-world environments. I have the privilege of having connections to the rest of the world.

Our business and daily life are often connected to our spiritual life. Deuteronomy 30:15 mentions 'land.' Verse 19 talks about life and our children. This is not just about us. This is for future generations. What are we doing for them?

All my grandchildren have their own Bibles. All parents should read the Bible to their children and pray for them more. I believe God has asked us to keep choosing the things that are right. The next generation is connected to our beliefs and God says He will give us many years in the land. There are always exceptions. During a time of intense favor, I had some family members fall ill, and during that time, my business was growing to the point that I had to hire one to two more people per month.

Every day I choose life and read Scriptures. I choose to make declarations of faith for many years in the land. Each morning, and sometimes during the mid-day, I read Scripture. I usually end the day with Scripture. I believe this makes a difference in my life. My brother, who was very ill, is now teaching a Bible study in a nursing home. There was a six-month period during which he could not talk.

Chapter 9: Men Behind the Vision: Adopting Behaviors & Expecting Impartation

He beat cancer despite nearly dying three times. Christian friends and my family agreed together for his healing several times. Hebrews 12:1-3 drives me to continue on. There are grandstands in heaven filled with people exhorting us on to victory. We must consider this so we do not grow weary.

The Lord continues to say, 'Trust Me.' Every day we have a chance to plant a seed of grace and speak a word from God to other people. I have come to realize that the only difference between misery and blessing is faith. Really, the same circumstances could happen to other people, but the difference lies in their reactions. Daniel 12: 3 reads, "Those who are wise will shine like the brightness of heaven." (7)

MaryAnn Maciag, New York

When my family was introduced to The Sowers Ministry, we immediately knew we had to become involved with this move of God. We agreed with the method of having native nationals presenting the gospel, and we started supporting those workers. Our confidence level increased when we learned Neil Anderson receives accountability reports from the pastors that he funds in ministry.

Working in countries where it is illegal to present the Word of God can bring about unusual, difficult, and sometimes even dangerous situations. Knowing Neil is a man of God who seeks the Holy Spirit's leading and direction made it an easier decision to back TSM. God is faithful to those who have not heard His truth and He proves this by raising up people to help the needy. There has been much fruit from the seeds that I have planted in this mission's ministry. It is very exciting to witness firsthand what God is doing. God will continue to bless the work of TSM because Neil answered the call of God and remains faithful. God has given us countless, creative ways to raise funds for believer's abroad.

R. Garnett, London, UK

Years ago, I read a quote from The Sowers Ministry about only 0.1% of the Church's wealth being used to reach the non-evangelized. For me, that was an eye-opener. I was both shocked and scandalized. The call of Christ is to reach the lost. My heart was saddened when I realized I was a part of the Western Church that was definitely not doing enough to reach those who need to hear the message of Jesus.

In that moment, I felt drawn to support Neil and TSM. It has been an extraordinary and exciting privilege to play even a very small part in what they have achieved. To see their impact, especially in Asia, has been amazing.

I am a businessman with no calling to the mission field. At times I wonder, "How can I, a middle-aged guy living a comfortable existence in Europe, live a life worthy of Christ's death and resurrection?" I believe part of the answer is in how I steward my money. God has blessed me richly so that I can know the joy of blessing others. That is where Neil and TSM come in. I know that my contributions, big or small, will go a very long way in his hands. I can barely wait to get to heaven to meet the hundreds of thousands of people touched and blessed by Sowers.

Neil is also a good friend whom I am honored to know. I cannot think of any other Christian leader who is more passionate about building a relationship with his supporters. To Neil and TSM it is less about the money and it is more about the relationships. I feel that is exactly how a ministry should be and how Jesus would have it.

Terry Chesbrough, Ft. Worth, Texas

In January of 1987, my wife and I moved to Hong Kong. It was there that we met three outstanding, young brothers. One of them was named Neil Anderson. Neil was incredibly hungry for the things of God. My wife and I showed him to pray the Word of God and to believe what the Scriptures say.

Chapter 9: Men Behind the Vision: Adopting Behaviors & Expecting Impartation

The more I explained to Neil the Word of God, the more the Lord began to expand the vision in Neil's heart. He began to desire to also do Christian work among the Vietnamese and Chinese people as well. Neil was committed to being mentored by me and the Holy Spirit. Whenever I would say let's pray, Neil would hit his knees in prayer even praying all night at times. Our time spent in prayer seeking God was one of supernatural encounters. We sought God and God then produced unlimited miracles such as increased finances to carry out the work of the ministry.

Over the years Neil Anderson and The Sowers Ministry has become a powerful force upon the earth for dispensing the gospel of Jesus Christ. When I partner with Neil, for the purpose of missions, the seeds I invest are multiplied a hundred times over. Ever since I met Neil I pray for him and the work he does on a daily basis.

Terry Barnett, Texas

Back in 1998, I was sitting in a Vietnamese restaurant reading a book about a great man of God. Suddenly, the Lord spoke to me and said, "Clean." This happened just as a man passed right next to my table. A few minutes later that man saw the title of the book I was reading, and commented about what a great man of God this person had been. I said, "Yes, you are right," and that began our conversation. Since then, our relationship has lasted for the past sixteen years!

We have continued to pray for Neil and his family and ministry. We have contributed to him with our love, encouragement and wisdom. We have also given financial gifts, especially to help provide Bibles in remotes countries of the Far East, where Bibles are not available or allowed.

Neil's work for the Lord is a huge undertaking. Neil's unique leadership style allows him to receive help from others and then turn around and give help to those who need it. Let us help him fulfill this great vision of end time sowing and reaping for God's kingdom.

Dr. Roger and Beverly Abel, Florida

As the old hymn goes, "We've a story to tell to the nations!" And, oh, what a story it is! A story of salvation, a story of healing, a story of deliverance, a story of prosperity, a story of being connected to our Father God through His Son, Jesus Christ, and a story of Holy Spirit revealing to us all that we actually are and have in Jesus -- a story of power and might! This story is too marvelous to put into meager words--it's a story that must be told, that must be received and that must be lived!

Jesus told us to go forth into all the world, and coupling that with Psalm 2:8, we had clear directions to go forth in His Name and in the power of the Holy Spirit into the nations and claim His possession for His Glory. Yes, we are able, and in Him we can do all things He declares that we should do. Point blank, we can, we are able because of all that He has done for us.

By the time we met Neil Anderson of The Sowers Ministry, we had already been going forth into the world for twelve years. We had preached in crusades in India and seen thousands saved and healed, we had already funded 2 orphanages in India, we had already preached about the Holy Spirit in Mexico and seen thousands receive the Baptism in the Holy Spirit, we had already funded feeding programs in Mexico. And though we were moving along at a good pace, we knew there was more, and as we were preaching and teaching in the Philippines, the Lord 'tweaked' our vision in a mighty way. Now was the time to go into China! "China? Are you kidding us?? We don't know anyone in China. You don't just walk into China and say here I am." "Are you able" questioned the Lord. "Yes, Master, we are able."

Chapter 9: Men Behind the Vision: Adopting Behaviors & Expecting Impartation

"Then I will make a way for you to get into China." Neil would be our way into China.

"Just blend in, Beverly, just blend in!" These are the words that Neil yelled to me over the heads of hundreds of Chinese who had rushed between us. As I watched Neil Anderson, my husband, Roger, and the rest of the team cross the border into China and walk out of sight, my prayer was, "Just blind their eyes, Father, just blind their eyes. There is no way my blond headed, blue-eyed, five foot nine inch frame can blend in with all these shorter, dark haired and dark eyed Chinese. Just blind their eyes and somehow get these suitcases filled with Bibles into China." And thus started our amazing, miraculous journey with Neil and TSM!

Roger and I immediately connected in spirit with Neil. Burning in all of us was the desire to get the Word of God into the nations! We met many more times in China, building relationships, preaching, teaching and always taking forth physically the written Word of God. The Bible says that there are no boundaries concerning the Word. We also find that in this period of God's amazing grace, we are ambassadors and we possess that divine immunity to go forth and connect nations with the Kingdom of God.

On one of our mission trips to the Philippines, the pastors there gave us an offering with this stipulation. "Please give this money to a pastor in another country who is going to plant a church. You have blessed us with the Word, now please bless someone on our behalf with this offering." After leaving Philippines, we went into China and met up with Neil. In a hotel in Shanghai, he introduced us to a pastor who was on his way to the northern part of China to plant a church. It was revealed in conversation that this Chinese pastor had the Bibles we had given him but no money to travel to the north. The Lord spoke to us to bless him with the offering. Some years later we found out that not only did this Chinese pastor plant a church, but thousands of souls had been saved through his ministry. He is still going strong today!

I must mention another special experience! We had just finished teaching a large group of church leaders and were preparing to anoint with oil, lay hands on them and pray for them. Earlier I had asked Neil to provide us with some oil, and he sent someone off to the store. When the time came for us to use the oil, each of us poured some in our hands from an attractive bottle with only Chinese writing on it. It went unnoticed that the cap of the bottle was pink! We immediately saw that this oil had a very strong smell and as we applied it to the hot, sweaty heads of the leaders, there appeared tiny bubbles! Bubbles, bubbles everywhere!! Panic followed! But in the end, it was a glorious time of anointing and praying. Who knows, perhaps that baby shampoo contained a little oil! Have you ever heard of Johnson and Johnson?

I would like to add, at this point, that the work in China continues, the story is still being told to the nation of China, and the Word of God is still going forth.

On one of Neil's visits to our home in Florida, he told us of his work in Ukraine. Immediately we knew our vision was being 'tweaked' again! By the time his visit was over, we had made plans with him to drive from Bern, Switzerland, 2700+ km all the way across Europe to the Southern part of Ukraine--to Izmail, Ukraine on the Danube River which empties into the Black Sea! For Neil, this was something he regularly did when not in Asia. For us, Europe was being opened to our ministry. Oh what a time we had! Supernatural all the way!! Neil loaded his SUV down with cold cuts, chips, bread, fruit, drinks and everything other kind of junk he could get his hands on. Did I forget the cookies? And off we went eating, laughing, praying, and trying to speak Russian by faith all the way to Izmail.

We have been several times to Ukraine with Neil. God has always moved in amazing ways in the lives of those we minister to and in our lives as well. We cherish our friends and all the children there. As well, we love and remember the church members in the churches that we are connected with.

Today, as Roger and I write this, Ukraine is experiencing a military incursion into their country by Russia. This, in turn, has caused severe economic situations in Izmail and nearby communities. Since our introduction to the Ukraine, we now are able to assist our friends and their churches with funds which are used to purchase food and other necessities. God loves Ukraine and God loves freedom. Russia! Let God's people go!

There are many, many more stories I could tell you, but since this is Neil's book, not ours, I will close with these thoughts. Our ministry parallels well with Neil's. It was the plan of God for each of our journeys that we should meet. We are 25 years older than Neil Anderson. He is like a very wise son to us, and it has been such a blessing to our lives to have this younger man's input. God has used Neil in our journey. And we have been used in his. Mutually, we pray for one another, we encourage one another, and we bounce ideas off of one another! In each nation we go into we take the gospel and the written Word of God, we know Neil has our back and we have his wherever he goes. We are looking forward to the next 'tweak' and to continued fellowship with TSM.

Dr. Paul Crites, Purpose International, TN

After investing time with Dr. Neil Anderson and learning of TSM's vision of touching lives and training leaders, I knew I had to partner with this ministry. My organization caught the concept of printing and placing Bibles in China and other regions of Asia. Each month I look forward to receiving Neil's updates on all the places TSM is taking the gospel.

Only one word is necessary to describe this organization and Neil's heart for the kingdom...*passion*. There are several groups doing many things in missions; however, like all things in life, it comes down to the leader, his life, and the vision. Dr. Neil Anderson and The Sowers Ministry are truly impacting the world for Christ and I am honored to be a part.

BIBLIOGRAPHY

1. http://dictionary.reference.com
2. http://en.wikipedia.org/wiki/Communication
3. *21 Things Every Leader Needs To Know* by Dr. Crites pgs. 4, 26, 34, 40, 42, 46, 48, 49, 65-66, 71, 73, 89, 104, 121.
4. *What Leaders Do: A Practical Guide to Developing Excellence in Leadership* by P.K.D. Lee, pgs. 14-15, 20, 21, 27, 35, 37...
5. *A Leader After God's Own Heart* – by Jim George, pgs. 34-37, 43, 74.
6. *Lead On!* By John Edmund Haggai pgs. 4, 6, 13, 17, 19, 24, 30, 37, 41, 104, 192.
7. www.Biblegateway.com, New International Version of *The Holy Bible*
8. *1599 Geneva Bible: Patriot's Edition* Tolle Lege Press & White Hall Press pg. xix
9. http://en.wikipedia.org/wiki/Cross-cultural_leadership
10. *Leading Cross-Culturally: Covenant Relationships for Effective Christian Leadership* By Sherwood G. Lingenfelter, back cover.
11. *The Mission Leadership Team* by David Mays
12. *Let the Sea Resound DVD Documentary* By The Sentinel Group (revivalworks.com)
13. *Humble is the Way* by David Jones, pgs. 195-204.
14. http://voices.yahoo.com/historys-famous-orphans-663015.html
15. *Jeffrey Gitomer's Little Black Book of Connections: 6.5 Assets for Networking Your Way to Rich Relationships* pgs 1-70
16. Ann Paedon, *A Strategy for Evangelization of Tibetan People in Tibet*, p. 45. Unpublished master's degree thesis.
17. *Asian Report*, October/November 1984 and July/August 1990.

18. *Tibetan Buddhism in America*, Pray for Tibet, Summer 1990.
19. *Tibet: Portrait of Change* and *Prayer Wheels & Red Meals*, Asiaweek, November 13, 1981.
20. *Unlocking the Mysteries of Tibet*, China and the Church Today, December 1985, p. 15.

www.ingramcontent.com/pod-product-compliance
Lightning Source LLC
LaVergne TN
LVHW051604070426
835507LV00021B/2756